Apocalypse Encrypted! Revelation Unleashed!

By:

Anthony Montoya

Apocalypse Encrypted!
Revelation Unleashed!

By

Anthony Montoya

Published By:

ABM Publications
A division of Andrew Bills Ministries Inc.
PO Box 6811, Orange, CA 92863

www.abmpublications.com

ISBN: 978-1-931820-56-1

DEDICATION

I would love to dedicate this book to my family & friends, who helped me through my walk of life. I would love to thank, David, Lupita, Nathaniel Sanchez & family, Pauli & Jack Taniguchi, My brothers Adrian Calderon and Robert Briseno for aiding me for shelter when I was living in my car. Also Prophet Mark, Sharon Sohmer, Mama McGee and Stevie. Prophetess Karen & Gilbert Bowser aiding me for shelter and food for several months. Prophetess Marie Santilliano for aiding me with intercession one night when I was in urgent need of a demonic attack, I was not supposed to be attending certain meetings where these spirits of warlocks and witches were even though they were apostles and prophets, I called Marie at midnight, I was being choked by a python spirit through a false prophet who astro projected out of his body and controlled another person to walk over to me and lay hands on me. She called it out within seconds and then rebuked me and corrected me. Prophetess Cynthia from Riverside California, Prophetess Cynthia from Glendale California. Prophetess Veronica from Rialto California, she called me one night while I was being attacked by the spirit of rejection & abandonment a dark heavy cloud, haven't spoke to her in three years and she called out of know where and broke the stronghold off me.

I would also like to thank, Prophetess Lily & Luis Avila, Sara, Denise, Prophet Brian & Claudia. Prophet Andre Hardin & Wife Pamela, Apostle Al Fornis for a major deliverance and breakthrough, Prophetess Deanne, Prophet Carlton LaGrange. Prophet Donnie from Louisiana who prophesied to me in detail and stated I had to wait 9 more months, and then I was removed from the burden of being homeless. Prophet Garret Lloyd, Prophet Michael Hodges & Family taking me through heavy healing and Deliverance. Prophet Hue Fortson taking me through heavy deliverance. Prophetess Stacy Yada, Apostle David Vizcara for aiding with money and material things. Prophet Alex & family, Prophetess Anita Morvac for her intercession, Prophetess Cindy from Upland California. Prophetess Young for her hospitality from Covina California. I would love to thank my brother Andrew from Corona California, Albert Garcia & family, Monique, Laura for aiding me food and money. Also I would love to thank Juan Valdez for shelter and food for several months. Prophet Evan walker for breaking a certain stronghold an affirming that it was over. My Parents Mary & Santiago for their tender loving care and hospitality.

SPECIAL APPRECIATION

I personally want to thank Bruce Dills and wife Shirley when I was homeless for shelter, food and aid. I also want to thank Gabriel Avila for his generous support funding Gods Kingdom, May Yeshua Increase and enlarge his Territory an End Time Prophet. I would also love to thank Ray Glory Ministries Prophetess Lilly Avila and Husband Prophet Mr. Burns. I would also love to thank Apostle Claudia and Prophet Brian Guerrero for making this happen, all their love and support. I would also love to Thank Apostle Sara Guerrero for her support and divine love and encouragement, a divine intercessor. I would also love to thank My Parents Mary & Santiago for all their hard work in everything they do. I would also love to thank my Publisher Andrew Bills and Family for His support.

TABLE OF CONTENTS

ACKNOWLEDGEMENTS

It is with much excitement and honor that I get the opportunity to acquaint you with my friend Anthony Montoya. In his unique style he reflects authentic leadership, tempered by a deep compassion for the lost. In this age of religious phonies and spiritual apathy, Anthony does not compromise the unfailing word of God.

His passion and exuberance for God is infectious; Challenging Christians to draw closer to God and take the Bible serious. During a time I was seeking a speaker for my Ministry, God said to me "call Anthony". God used Anthony to confirm some important future Ministry events that He had already spoken to me about. For the reasons above, and others that followed, I look forward to future Ministry with Anthony where his gifts will edify and be a blessing to the Body of Christ.

Lilly Avila
Rays of Glory Ministries, Inc.

In all the 19 years that I have known Anthony Montoya, he has been very poised and consistent. He's a man I know who rightly divides the Word of truth. He carefully hears from the Holy Spirit and he speaks as the Spirit gives him the utterance. I highly recommend his work to any reader out there.

Lloyd Nsek
Author of *"Christianity the End of Spiritual Confusion"*

CHAPTER 1

Revelation 101, continuing specified instructions of service to Yahweh our Father. His Holy Spirit the Baptism of Fire burns out carnality intrusions (An **intrusion** is liquid rock that forms under Earth's surface. <u>Magma</u> from under the surface is slowly pushed up from deep within the earth into any cracks or spaces it can find, sometimes pushing existing <u>country rock</u> out of the way, a process that can take millions of years. As the rock slowly cools into a solid, the different parts of the magma <u>crystallize</u> into minerals). You notice within your spirits you have been impregnated with poisoned eggs within your spirit that went so deep into your heart, body, mind, soul & spirit woven like thread and creates a solid form of instructions. Basically you're malfunctioning inaccurately instead of being freed or loosed from witchery. Psalms 58 Do ye indeed speak righteousness, O congregation? Do ye judge uprightly, O ye sons of men? [2] Yea, in heart ye work wickedness; ye weigh the violence of your hands in the earth.[3] The wicked are estranged from the womb: they go astray as soon as they be born, speaking lies.[4] Their poison is like the poison of a serpent: they are like the deaf adder that stoppeth her ear.

Now more information of rain revelations, Psalms 111:5 ([5] He has given food *and* provision to those who reverently *and* worship fully fear Him; He will remember His covenant forever *and* imprint it [on His mind]. Now if you remember in my recent books about (Tithe) one portion of a whole Complete Reverence. (Part of us that's sanctified to become apostolic and a portion that is set aside for you (Soul Mate). Yahweh took out one rib a portion of himself to create Woman Eve. The human has 24 ribs 12 on each side. Revelation 21: 12 And had a wall great and high, and had twelve gates, and at the gates twelve angels, and names written thereon, which are the names of the twelve tribes of the children of Israel: 13 On the east three gates; on the north three gates; on the south three gates; and on the west three gates.14 And the wall of the city had twelve foundations, and in them the names of the twelve apostles of the Lamb. Rib in Hebrew means a chamber of cells. The father wants his complete dominion and authority within us. Revelation 4 verse 1 After this I looked, and, behold, a door was opened in heaven: and the first voice which I heard was as it were of a trumpet talking with me; which said, Come up hither, and I will shew thee things which must be hereafter. There 12 gates, 12 angels, 12 tribes, 12 foundations equals 48, which is symbolic of the 48 prophets of the Old testament. 1) Abraham2) Isaac3) Jacob4) Moses5) Aaron6) Joshua7) Pinchas the High Priest8) Elkanah (father of Samuel)9) Eli the High Priest10) Samuel11) Gad12) Nathan13) King David14) King Solomon15) Eido16) Michiyahu ben Yimlah17) Obadiah18) Achiyah of Shiloh19) Yahu ben Chanani20) Azariah ben Oded21) Chaziel son of Metaniah22) Eliezer of Morisha23) Hosea24) Amos25) Micah26) Amotz27) Elijah28) Elisha29) Jonah30) Isaiah31) Joel32) Nahum33) Habakkuk34) Zephaniah35) Uriah from Kiryat Yearim36) Jeremiah37) Ezekiel38) Shmaya39) Baruch40) Neriah41) Seriah42) Mechasiah43) Haggai 44) Zechariah45) Malachi46) Mordechai47) Chanani48) Oded. Trumpets are the prophets speaking to us!

2 And immediately I was in the spirit: and, behold, a throne was set in heaven, and one sat on the throne.3 And he that sat was to look upon like a jasper and a sardine stone: and there was a rainbow round about the throne, in

sight like unto an emerald.4 And round about the throne were four and twenty seats: and upon the seats I saw four and twenty elders sitting, clothed in white raiment; and they had on their heads crowns of gold. So there is 24 elders sitting down reigning with Yeshua death is swallowed up in victory (complete dominion). We have 24 ribs, 12 tribes of Israel which are also foundations (Authority) and the 12 apostles (Dominion). , 5 And out of the throne proceeded lightning's and thundering's and voices: and there were seven lamps of fire burning before the throne, which are the seven Spirits of God. How many prophetess were there in the bible, 7 women prophetess which resembles the menorah, the book of proverbs speaks of a woman which is wisdom. The seven lampstands which is the Menorah. Christ (To sit means Dominion, enemies under your feet). Jasper in Hebrews yashepheh- means to polish to shine. Rainbow in Hebrew Qeshet, God's forgiveness and his covenantal mercy. Emerald in Hebrew nophek: (a precious stone) perhaps emerald which is a symbolic of wealth to Honor the King Yeshua! White raiment in Hebrew leukos of white garments as the sign of innocence and purity of the soul. Gold in Hebrew kethem, something carved out or wedged, refined through the fire. The lamb stand, the seven spirits of Yahweh within us, also it's the Menorah, the candles which was in the inner court of the tabernacle. Its resemblance is the church age here and now. In Hebrew elder means Ancient man, the prophets and the apostles that passed the test and were refined sitting on thrones reigning with Christ.

The 12 tribes names=Judah means-Praise, Reuben-behold a son he looks upon me (affliction, Gad-troop or fortune, Asher-Happy, Naphtali-my wrestling and strife, Manasseh-

making me to forget-Debt free all my troubles, Simeon - God hears me being an agreement(heard that I am unloved), Levi- joined me unity attached, Issachar-purchased me recompense (wages), Zebulun-habitation dwelling(good gift), Joseph- God will add increase inheritance(taken away my reproach), Benjamin-Son of many sorrows became son of his right hand Power. The Apostles names Simeon-God has heard, Peter-Rock the gates of hell shall not prevail, Andrew-manly new man, John-God is gracious, James- Israel one who supplants his brother, Thomas-spiritual likeness, Matthew-Gift of God, Bartholomew-Son of Talmai, Talmai is a Canaanite giant in Numbers 13:22-Talmai is king of Geshur, one of David's fathers in law-Numbers 13-33 33 And there we saw the giants, the sons of Anak, which come of the giants: and we were in our own sight as grasshoppers, and so we were in their sight-2 Samuel 3:3 2 And unto David were sons born in Hebron: and his firstborn was Amnon, of Ahinoam the Jezreelitess;3 And his second, Chileab, of Abigail the wife of Nabal the Carmelite; and the third, Absalom the son of Maacah the daughter of Talmai king of Geshur. Judas-Praise or praised one, Phillip-lover of horses, Thaddeus Gift of God, Paul (Shaul)- ask of (Yah) first king.

Revelation 4 verse 6 And before the throne there was a sea of glass like unto crystal: and in the midst of the throne, and round about the throne, were four beasts full of eyes before and behind. What's 12 divided by 48 it equals 4. 7 And the first beast was like a lion, and the second beast like a calf, and the third beast had a face as a man, and the fourth beast was like a flying eagle.8 And the four beasts had each of them six wings about him; and they were full of eyes within: and they rest not day and night, saying, Holy, holy, holy, LORD God Almighty, which was, and is, and is to come. These are the resemblance of the seraphim's and cherubim's angels. So Yahweh is saying who becomes the seraphim's and the cherubim's us, Elijah out ran chariots, 1 Kings 18:46 Then the LORD gave special strength to Elijah. He tucked his cloak into his belt and ran ahead of Ahab's chariot all the way to the entrance of Jezreel. The Lion of the tribe of Judah (Yeshua lion) - Calf (Lamb Sacrifice), Man- Human (Us), Flying Eagle (Vision in the spirit). Isaiah 40:31 but they that wait upon the LORD shall renew *their* strength; they shall mount up with wings as eagles; they shall run, and not be weary; *and* they shall walk, and not faint.

Revelation chap 7:3 Saying, Hurt not the earth, neither the sea, nor the trees, till we have sealed the servants of our God in their foreheads.4 And I heard the number of them which were sealed: and there were sealed an hundred and forty and four thousands of all the tribes of the children of Israel. This number is talking about the 144,000, what this symbolically means you say. Saints listen carefully, 12 tribes of Israel and the 12Foundations, 12x12 equals 144 x 1,000 years reign with Christ equals 144,000. It is a love letter to the Bride, we are entering a marriage feast with him to be united as one! I will praise the lord for he has looked on me and granted good fortune. I am happy because of my wrestling, God is making me to forget. God hears me and is joined to me. He has purchased me a dwelling and will add to me, the son of his right hand. Praise confession of the letter, Behold, a son, a whole troop whose fortune has come. They are happy and blessed after wrestling and striving, forgetting their past troubles, hearing and obeying, united as one. Their recompense for their labor is to dwell with God, and he will Increase and add to them many sons of His right hand.

"This time I will praise the lord. Because the lord has seen my affliction, surely now my husband will love me (First Son. How fortunate! Happy am I! For women will call me happy. With might wrestling's I have wrestled with my sister, and I have indeed prevailed. God has made me forget all my troubles and all my father's household. Because the lord has heard that I am unloved, He has therefore given me this (Second) son also. Now this time my husband will become attached to me, because I have borne him three sons. God has given me my wages because I gave my maid to my husband. God has endowed me with a good gift; now my husband will dwell with me, because I have borne him six (six) sons. God has taken away my reproach. May the Lord give me another son (Seventh)? The son of my sorrows has become the son (Eighth) of my right hand.'

Revelation 21:21 And I saw a new heaven and a new earth: for the first heaven and the first earth were passed away; and there was no more sea.2 And I John saw the holy city, new Jerusalem, coming down from God out of heaven, prepared as a bride adorned for her husband (Married to his Shekinah glory being united with him in the Holy Holies.3 And I heard a great voice out of heaven saying, Behold, the tabernacle of God is with men(Tabernacle) us him within us, united as one, and he will dwell with them, and they shall be his people, and God himself shall be with them, and be their God.4 And God shall wipe away all tears from their eyes; and there shall be no more death, neither sorrow, nor crying, neither shall there be any more pain: for the former things are passed away.5 And he that sat upon the throne said, Behold, I make all things new. And he said unto me, write: for these words are true and faithful.6 and he said unto me, it is done. I am Alpha and

Omega, the beginning and the end. I will give unto him that is athirst of the fountain of the water of life freely (The Gift of Immortality).7 He that overcometh shall inherit all things; and I will be his God, and he shall be my son. Those who have completely come to the end of self shall inherit all things! You notice verse 21 states there was no more sea, the sea is no longer to be searched out meaning his knowledge, and it states in the word the knowledge of Yahweh shall cover like the waters of the sea. Well when we come into immortality or perfection we become the sea.

Eyeh Asher Eyeh speaks to us when his son is returning for us, Genesis 1:16 And God made the two great lights—the greater light (the sun) to rule the day and the lesser light (the moon) to rule the night. He also made the stars.17 And God set them in the expanse of the heavens to give light upon the earth, 18 to rule over the day and over the night, and to separate the light from the darkness. And God saw that it was good (fitting, pleasant) *and* He approved it.19 and there was evening and there was morning, a fourth day. Yeshua is the son of God, Yeshua is the circle of the feasts around the moon or the moon feasts, and He is the bright and morning star. Revelation 22:16 "I, Jesus, have sent my angel to give you this testimony for the churches. I am the Root and the Offspring of David, and the bright Morning Star." Psalm 83:3 Sound the ram's horn at the New Moon, and when the moon is full, on the day of our festival. "'And it shall come to pass that from one New Moon to another, and from one Sabbath to another, all flesh shall come to worship before Me,' says the Lord." (Isaiah 66:23, NKJV). Yah says my son shall return on the 4day which is 4,000 years. It states one day is like a thousand years to Yah. The

Tabernacle explained, Outer court 1500 cubits, 1500 years from the time Moses went to the mountain to receive the opening of the Veils to meet with an Angel of Yahweh(Apocalypse- Apo's to open, Kolyptos in Hebrew and Greek means the opening of the veils). Inner court measurements 10x20x10 equals=2,000 years from the time Yeshua died on the Cross. This is the church age the bride preparing for the marriage feast. The Holy Holies its measurements are 10x10x10 which means and equals 1,000 years. We are in 2,014 today, then what's the third day, we are entering into then. The 3rd day is the 1,000 years of reigning with Christ here and now in our immortal glorified bodies. When we end up after one more 1,000 years it will be 3,014 which steps into the 4th day. When 3,000 ends up and then becomes one more day into the 3,001 it's considered the 4th day.

Genesis 3:24 So [God] drove out the man; and He placed at the east of the Garden of Eden the [c]cherubim and a flaming sword which turned every way, to keep *and* guard the way to the tree of life. Unity means in Hebrew to be joined together when the speaker and the receiver touch and agree, its two parallel lines that come to a point, which resembles a sword. Hebrews 4:12 for the word of God *is* quick, and powerful, and sharper than any two edged sword, piercing even to the dividing asunder of soul and spirit, and of the joints and marrow, and *is* a discerner of the thoughts and intents of the heart. Sword of truth, is the word of Yahweh which is also his Secrets and mysteries revealed only by His Apostles and Prophets. So if the veils are being opened and we receive the secrets and mysteries and of course coming to the end of ourselves we are entering back into the Garden of Eden. Flaming in Ancient Hebrew lexicon means opening veils mysteries and secrets.

CHAPTER 2

What is the story or love letter? What significance are interwoven in this statement? First, it begins and ends with a good them. It starts with praising the lord and ends with a son of my right hand.

The hand signifies (Power) and the right hand signifies (Eminent) or (Divine) power." Yeshua is now seated at the right hand of God (Mark 16:19, Acts 2:33). Stephen, being full of the Holy Spirit, saw Yeshua standing at the right hand of God (Acts 7:55). In his Patmos vision, John saw Yeshua holding seven stars in his right hand (Revelation 1:16). Further, the right hand was always used when a patriarch wanted to bestow a special blessing on a son, especially one being afforded the blessings of the inheritance of a firstborn (Genesis 48:14).

Second, son ship is the central them. Son ship is all about maturing from a child of God into a son of God, and this comes about through spiritual perfection that is ultimately manifested through resurrection and transfiguration and into an immortal, glorified, spiritual, celestial body in the image of the son of God. This speaks of the 8th day, which is the resurrection day. When we first believe, we are born from above with the seed of God residing within us (1 John 3:9), but this seed must grow and mature until one day it births the new man in us. 9 No one born (begotten) of God [deliberately, knowingly, and [h]habitually] practices sin, for God's nature abides in him [His principle of life, the divine sperm, remains permanently within him]; and he cannot practice sinning because he is born (begotten) of God.

Technically, all believers are sons of God, but the question of when one will be manifested as a son depends on being counted worthy of the kingdom and glory (1 Thessalonians 2:12). All will be in glory in Gods day. The question is who will reign with Christ in the age to come or the Lords Day or the Day of Christ (Kingdom Age, Tabernacle Age,). Only those who conquer (Overcome) will be counted worthy to enter Eon age (Forever-Agelessness and Immortal life to reign with Christ, both in the earthly and heavenly realms, for 1,000 years. The rest of the dead will not come to life until the end of the 1,000 years (Revelation 20:4-6), saved yet so as through fire (1 Corinthians 3:15). The above scriptural statement reveals a very important point regarding what it takes to be a conqueror, and it is discovered in the prophetic meanings of the 7th and 8th names listed. I am speaking of the love letter which was a few paragraphs above. Clearly, there are 12 sons in view in the statement, but notice that three sons, then six sons, then another son, and then finally a son of my right hand are mentioned, and is this order. In other words, the number of sons builds until what appears to be 8 sons not 12. Another son and the son of my right hand would presumably be the 7th and 8th sons respectively in the love letter. This might seem strange but perhaps is by design. Between Leah and Rachel, the two free wives of Jacob, were 8 sons, 6 from Leah's womb and 2 from Rachel's womb. However, special note needs to be made that it is not until after stating "God has taken away my reproach" that the 7th and 8th sons come into view. In other words, Reproach must be removed before the last two of the eight sons come forth. The numbers alone are prophetically significant. The number 7 signifies "spiritual perfection" and the number 8 "new birth, new creation, or new beginnings." God rest on the 7th day of creation. What's the

8th day then, a new book is being written, we shall do greater works then Yeshiva for now he goes onto the Father, The Holy of Holies in the Tabernacle to become one and unite with him.

You notice in the love letter in the 12 tribes it ends up with the 7th and 8th tribe, 8th God hears me, hearing, obeying and being an agreement, levy joined to me, joiner, adhesion unification to become one. Technically in the love letter the 7th and 8th son become the right hand of power! Benjamin: son of the Right hand. Just as joseph is a type of Christ so is Benjamin a type. Yeshua is at the right hand of God the father (Acts7:55-56), and he has called and chosen a company of conquerors to do likewise in the next age (New world). Further, just as joseph's birth order is significant so is Benjamin's birth order, for he was the eighth and last son of the two free wives. As previously shown, the number eight signifies a new birth or new creation. Surely, the Conquerors are the First fruits of the New Creation. They are the saints through whom the lord will judge the world and the angels (1 Corinthians 6:2-3) According to his fiery law. 2 Do you not know that the saints (the believers) will [one day] judge *and* govern the world? And if the world [itself] is to be judged *and* ruled by you, are you unworthy *and* incompetent to try [such petty matters] of the smallest courts of justice?3 Do you not know also that we [Christians] are to judge the [very] angels *and* pronounce opinion between right and wrong [for them]? How much more then [as to] matters pertaining to this world *and* of this life only!

It states and one sat on the throne which was Yeshua. "And thou shalt set in it [the high-priest's breastplate] settings of stones, even four rows of stones: the first row shall be a sardius, a topaz, and a carbuncle: this shall be the first row. And the second row shall be an emerald, a sapphire, and a diamond. And the third row a ligure, an agate, and an amethyst. And the fourth row a beryl, and an onyx, and a jasper: they shall be set in gold in their enclosing's" -- Exodus 28:17-20. You notice that's twelve stones representing the 12 tribes of Israel. You notice There are 3stones missing from Satan, Satan originally had 12stones. The truth and opposite of Satan's stones, Ruby-Rueben-submission >Rebellion, Topaz Simeon-Pure > Unclean, Beryl-Levi to give light > darkness ignorance, Turquoise-Judah law of Yahweh > no law, Sapphire -Dan-Book of Yahweh > 2/3 missing, Emerald-To heal-Naphtali >sickness disease, Chrysoline-Zebulun-reverence > irreverence, Onyx- Joseph-zeal > Luke warmness, Jasper-tribe Benjamin-Yahweh is our strength (Thy will be done) > self-will your own strength.

3 stones missing, Name of Yahweh Jacinth-Gad Authority, Agate-Asher to restore return repent, The Amethyst-Yissachar Unity. The book of Daniel 12 verse 7 And I heard the man clothed in linen, who was above the waters of the river, when he held up his right and his left hand toward the heavens and swore by Him Who lives forever that it shall be for a time, times, and a half a time [or three and one-half years]; and when they have made an end of shattering *and* crushing the power of the holy people, all these things shall be finished. It specifically states 3 ½ years which equals 3,500 years. Outer court 1500 years, Inner court 10x20x10=2,000 years from Yeshua dying on the cross it comes to an end. The next age or new world is the Kingdom age The Tabernacle age. Saints Satan is a symbol of 1/3 meaning The father Son Holy Spirit are one he has been severed and cut off/ three signifies three, Me Myself

& I attitude. Revelation 12:4 Rev. 12:4, "And his tail swept away a third of the stars of heaven, and threw them to the earth. And the dragon stood before the woman who was about to give birth, so that when she gave birth he might devour her child."

Saints what's 1/3 of five is 1.66, what's the Mark of the Beast 666, Satan has two sides The Most Beautiful Angel and the Angel of Light Spirit, 66 means double figure, double minded and Deceitful. In order for him to become one his twisted thinking and ignorance and carnal understanding he need another number 6,666 the number of man's what's 6+6=12 stones or the Twelve tribes of Israel, Do not cast your fruit to the ground, or you will lose your unity, your authority and you will not Bear the Mark of the name of Yahweh on your forehead. The symbolic meaning Satan the Fallen angel which once had 12stones 6+6 equals 12. If you turn the 66 number upside down it resembles a 99 which now Satan only has 9 stones also reverence of truth and false. Furthermore Satan stated I shall be greater than the Most High, He thought as himself Almost Perfect about 99 percent. Only Yahweh is 100 percent all in all!

The Mark of the beast explained 666 in the above paragraph when you do not repent, so if you repent and untwist your thinking and become opposite of 666, which then becomes 999. What's 9x3 equals 27 or 9+9+9 which equals 27. Revelation 4 verse 4 stated there was 24 elders of the Sanhedrin reigning with Christ Yeshua. The symbolic meaning those who overcomes shall rule and reign in the new Kingdom age, Tabernacle age 24 elders reigning with who Father, Son, Holy Spirit which is 3 more which are one, which makes 27. The father is Sovereign last say so, The

Son his grace, The Holy Spirit has the rod or whip or with love. Some of you may ask why 1/3 of five, Satan is against the Apostolic. Yeshua says be sharp as a serpent and soft as a dove, the dove has five pinons on his tail which resembles fivefold ministry, the dove is symbolic of the Holy Spirit.

Daniel 12 verse 11 And from the time that the continual burnt offering is taken away and the abomination that makes desolate is set up, there shall be 1,290 days. What is 1+2+9 equals 12 which resembles the 12 tribes of Israel placing12 in front of 0, equals 120. It took Noah 120 years to build an ark. It says Abomination means a thing that causes discuss or hatred, the wicked, desolate means a laid waste-dismal emptiness. Yah dismissed the wicked from the earth and made it treeless. This also means we need to empty ourselves wholeheartedly completely. The zero resembles emptiness, selfless, dying to self completely.

Daniel 12: 12 Blessed, happy, fortunate, spiritually prosperous, *and* to be envied is he who waits expectantly *and* earnestly [who endures without wavering beyond the period of tribulation] and comes to the 1,335 days! Speaking of a point time in a mystery secret, He begins speaking about the tribes of Israel, Blessed (Praise) was Judah=Happy was Asher=Fortunate was Gad=Spiritually Prosperous was Joseph. Now what's the secret of these days, the twelve tribes of Israel also, 1+3+3+5 equals 12. Furthermore 1,335 minus 1,290 days equals 45. It took Moses people 4o years to enter into the Promised Land, five means fivefold ministry, 4o is also the symbolic of it took 4o years to get Egypt the abomination and the desolation out of them. How long did It rain when got flooded the earth , Genesis 7:4 For yet seven days, and I

16

will cause it to rain upon the earth forty days and forty nights; and every living substance that I have made will I destroy from off the face of the earth.

Saints the number 40 also resembles a cleansing process cleaning out all the impurities and come to the end of self. The church must accept my Principles of Fivefold Ministry and rightful order. They must accept the Apostolic within them to be birthed out. They must accept and receive my secrets and mysteries to receive. The five represents the apostolic ministry, fivefold ministry which we all know worldwide it's rejected in most religions.

Revelation 2:17 He who is able to hear, let him listen to *and* heed what the Spirit says to the assemblies (churches). To him who overcomes (conquers), I will give to eat of the manna that is hidden, and I will give him a white stone with a new name engraved on the stone, which no one knows *or* understands except he who receives it. [26] And he who overcomes (is victorious) and who obeys My commands to the [very] end [doing the works that please Me], I will give him authority *and* power over the nations; [27] And he shall rule them with a scepter (rod) of iron, as when earthen pots are broken in pieces, and [his power over them shall be] like that which I Myself have received from My Father;

1 Corinthians 15:49 And just as we have borne the image [of the man] of dust, so shall we *and so* [g]*let us* also bear the image [of the Man] of heaven.[50] But I tell you this, brethren, flesh and blood cannot [become partakers of eternal salvation and] inherit *or* share in the kingdom of God; nor does the perishable (that which is decaying) inherit *or* share in the imperishable (the immortal).[51] Take notice! I tell you a mystery (a secret truth, an event

decreed by the hidden purpose or counsel of God). We shall not all fall asleep [in death], but we shall all be changed (transformed)

[52] In a moment, in the twinkling of an eye (Atoms atomic levels two atoms need to Unite) as one), at the [sound of the] last trumpet call. For a trumpet will sound, and the dead [in Christ] will be raised imperishable (free and immune from decay), and we shall be changed (transformed).

[53] For this perishable [part of us] must put on the imperishable [nature], and this mortal [part of us, this nature that is capable of dying] must put on immortality (freedom from death).

[54] And when this perishable puts on the imperishable and this that was capable of dying puts on freedom from death, then shall be fulfilled the Scripture that says, Death is swallowed up (utterly vanquished [h]forever) in and unto victory. Immortality.

Philippians 3:21 [21] Who will [a]transform and fashion anew the body of our humiliation to conform to and be like the body of His glory and majesty, by exerting that power which enables Him even to subject everything to Himself.

Romans 8: [29] For those whom He foreknew [of whom He was [k]aware and [l]loved beforehand], He also destined from the beginning [foreordaining them] to be molded into the image of His Son [and share inwardly His likeness], that He might become the firstborn among many brethren. [30] And those whom He thus foreordained, He also called; and those whom He called, He also justified (acquitted, made righteous, putting them into right standing with Himself). And those whom He justified, He also glorified [raising them to a heavenly dignity and condition or state of being].Immortality.

Psalms 17:15 [15] As for me, I will continue beholding Your face in righteousness (rightness, justice, and right standing with You); I shall be fully satisfied, when I awake [to find myself] beholding Your form [and having sweet communion with You]. His exact likeness.

Romans 6: [4] Therefore we are buried with Him by baptism into death, that just as Christ was raised up from the dead by the glory of the Father, even so we also should walk in newness of life. [5] For if we have been planted together in the likeness of His death, so we shall also be in the likeness of His resurrection,

2 Corinthians 3: [10] Indeed, in view of this fact, what once had splendor [[c]the glory of the Law in the face of Moses] has come to have no splendor at all, because of the overwhelming glory that exceeds *and* excels it [[d]the glory of the Gospel in the face of Jesus Christ]. [11] For if that which was but passing *and* fading away came with splendor, how much more must that which remains *and* is permanent abide in glory *and* splendor! [12] Since we have such [glorious] hope (such joyful and confident expectation), we speak very freely *and* openly *and* fearlessly. [13] Nor [do we act] like Moses, who put a veil over his face so that the Israelites might not gaze upon the finish of the vanishing [splendor which had been upon it]. [14] In fact, their minds were grown hard *and* calloused [they had become dull and had lost the power of understanding]; for until this present day, when the Old Testament (the old covenant) is being read, that same veil still lies [on their hearts], not being lifted [to reveal] that in Christ it is made void *and* done away. [15] Yes, down to this [very] day whenever Moses is

read, a veil lies upon their minds *and* hearts.[16] But whenever a person turns [in repentance] to the Lord, the veil is stripped off *and* taken away.[17] Now the Lord is the Spirit, and where the Spirit of the Lord is, there is liberty (emancipation from bondage, freedom).[18] And all of us, as with unveiled face, [because we] continued to behold [in the Word of God] as in a mirror the glory of the Lord, are constantly being transfigured into His *very own* image in ever increasing splendor *and* from one degree of glory to another; [for this comes] from the Lord [Who is] the Spirit.

Luke 4: [33] and they rose up that same hour and returned to Jerusalem, and found the eleven gathered together and those who were with them, [34] saying, "The Lord is risen indeed and hath appeared to Simon!"[35] And they told what things were done on the way, and how He was known to them in the breaking of bread.[36] and as they thus spoke, Jesus Himself stood in the midst of them and said unto them, "Peace be unto you."[37] But they were terrified and afraid, and supposed that they had seen a spirit.[38] And He said unto them, "Why are ye troubled, and why do thoughts arise in your hearts? [39] Behold My hands and my feet, that it is I Myself. Handle Me and see, for a spirit hath not flesh and bones, as ye see me to have."[40] And when He had thus spoken, He showed them His hands and His feet.[41] And while they yet believed not for joy, and wondered, He said unto them, "Have ye here any meat?"[42] And they gave Him a piece of a broiled fish and of a honeycomb. [43] And He took it and ate before them.[44] And He said unto them, "These are the words which I spoke unto you while I was yet with you, that all things must be fulfilled which were written in the Law of Moses and in the Prophets and in the Psalms concerning Me."[45] Then opened He their understanding, that they might understand the Scriptures, [46] and said unto them, "Thus it is written, and thus it behooved Christ to suffer and to rise from the dead the third day,

2 Corinthians 5:5 For we know that if our earthly house, this tabernacle, were dissolved, we have a building of God, a house not made with hands, eternal in the heavens. [2] For in this we groan, earnestly desiring to be clothed about with our house which is from Heaven, [3] that, being so clothed, we shall not be found naked. [4] For we that are in this tabernacle do groan, being burdened, not because we would be unclothed, but clothed about, that mortality might be swallowed up by life. Heaven is as most view, is not our hope. A glorified immortal body is our hope, to be clothed in our dwelling out of heaven, then this mortal is swallowed by life! Christ in us the hope of Glory!

Acts 8: [38] and he commanded the chariot to stand still, and they both went down into the water, both Philip and the eunuch, and he baptized him. [39] and when they had come up out of the water, the Spirit of the Lord caught away Philip. And the eunuch saw him no more, and went on his way rejoicing. [40] But Philip was found at Azotus, and passing through, he preached in all the cities until he came to Caesarea. He was transferred in spirit.

Colossians 1: [26] The mystery of which was hidden for ages and generations [[x]from angels and men], but is now revealed to His holy people (the saints), [27] To whom God was pleased to make known how great for the Gentiles are the riches of the glory of this mystery, which is Christ within *and* among you, the Hope of [realizing the] glory.

"In Exodus 28, we read of these stones in the breastplate of the high priest. The Sardius (the blood-red) stone having to do with Reuben is mentioned first, and the Jasper stone last. Revelation 4 speaks first of the Jasper stone--the clear white stone of Benjamin. This is not to be taken lightly. There is a definite reason for reversing of the stones, putting the first last, and the last first.

"The Sardius was blood-red, speaking of the sacrifice of blood, pointing to the cross and the first coming of Jesus to shed His blood for the remission of sin. The name is derived from two Hebrew words meaning 'behold the Son.' It pointed to the person of whom John the Baptist said, 'Behold the Lamb of God which taketh away the sin of the world' (John 1:29). It also tells us that He (the Lord Jesus) was the first born of every creature, and the first begotten--the ONLY begotten--son of God (John 3:16).

"The Jasper, the last stone in the Old Testament breastplate, represented Benjamin. This was a clear stone, speaking of total victory. On the Jasper stone was Benjamin's name, which is a combination of two Hebrew words (BEN and JAMIN), so scholars tell us, meaning 'the son of my right hand'...or, as one authority puts it, 'the son of my power.' The first and last stones pointed forward to the first and second coming of the great High Priest--none other than the Lord Jesus Christ.

"However, here in Revelation 4, the order of the stones is reversed. John the Beloved sees Him (Jesus) first as the Jasper, and second as the Sardius. The reason is clear: In the Old Testament the saints looked forward to the day when the Lamb would come, they looked forward to the cross, and therefore saw the Sardius...the blood-red stone...first. They looked beyond that and saw the Jasper, the clear white stone representing His power and His rule at His second coming to set up the kingdom. However, when John had the experience we are now studying, he was on this side of Calvary and the Rapture, and was looking back. John saw, first of all, the Jasper stone, the clear one--and then the red stone, the cross and sacrifice."

Amos 9:6English Standard Version (ESV) 6 who builds his upper chambers in the heavens and founds his vault upon the earth; who calls for the waters of the sea and pours them out upon the surface of the earth—the LORD is his name. He Yahweh builds his upper chambers, within us created in the likeness of the fabrication of his framework. It continues to say his vault upon the earth, sealed and hidden stored away within us upon this earth which is us human. Who calls forth the waters, The Holy spirit of him within us stirring up the gifts and talents, the sea, his knowledge and understanding, his revelation and his mysteries? What's hidden within a vault it's a mystery, you need a key or code for it to be unlocked. Chamber in Hebrew cheder means bedroom, intimacy, spend time with him alone. Ecclesiastes 8:3 do not be in a hurry to leave the king's presence. Do not stand up for a bad cause, for he will do whatever he pleases. Vault in Hebrew means, circle, circuit, compass, circle means whole all of him, circuit means energy life source of regeneration, compass means navigation, has also to do with his timing. There is a height, length and a depth of him. How high up it goes to know him and reach him is a nonstop process forever reaching him, how long it is ongoing road of secrets, depth how deep is his love.

Offering (Sacrifice), you become the sacrifice of worship unto him whole heartedly. You notice pagan's and occults when there is a sacrifice ceremony going on theirs usually a form of worship dance that goes along with it. Hello Saints we were created to dance before him in spirit and truth, now let me give you some understanding. Those of you who desire a wife or husband what usually goes on in the privacy of your own bedroom (Yea a Rodeo demonstration). When it comes to worship the Heavenly father you love so much you can't or won't move a muscle and just very moderately clap or sing with 30 percent or 5o percent exhaustion.

Psalms 111:10 ([10] The reverent fear *and* worship of the Lord is the beginning of [a]Wisdom *and* skill [the preceding and the first essential, the prerequisite and the alphabet]; a good understanding, wisdom, *and* meaning have all those who do [the will of the Lord]. Their praise of Him endures forever. What he speaks of and you allow his meat of the word, rain revelation saturate you, it becomes which is states the beginning of wisdom and essential skilled practice. Practice worshiping him, whole heartedly, obey and do his will first.

CHAPTER 3

My beloved saints, the spirit of religion is very demonic and deceitful and sometimes beyond the human comprehension. Let me give you some illustration what ails you to think in such a manner and form. The book of Galatians chap 4 verse 7 Therefore, you are no longer a slave (bond servant) but a son; and if a son, then [it follows that you are] an heir [c]by the aid of God, *through Christ*.8 But at that previous time, when you had not come to be acquainted with *and* understand *and* know the true God, you [Gentiles] were in bondage to gods who by their very nature could not be gods at all [gods that really did not exist].9 Now, however, that you have come to be acquainted with *and* understand *and* know [the true] God, or rather to be understood *and* known by God, how can you turn back again to the weak and beggarly *and* worthless elementary things [[d]of all religions before Christ came], whose slaves you once more want to become?10 You observe [particular] days and months and seasons and years!

This injunction of insight also speaks of the logical, analytical comprehension of common sense! 1. Who 2. What 3. When 4. Where 5 .Why & the 6. How benefactor. You were raised this way in your society, the beastly mentality of mankind is 666. Number six is the way of preparation, we need to come out of this logic and understanding. In all my years of Ministry service this stronghold still within almost everyone, I continue to be acquainted with lives in these web filters. We to unveil the Mystery Revelations of secrets of understanding prophetically what the word is saying. You all actually believe there is Miracles in God and call it a miracle. Yahshua the prophets & apostles walked in this normality of state of condition in the awe and the by nature how we were once created. It's a normal thing to believe and know, understand and comprehend all things are possible. It is our normal state to walk how our King Walked Yeshua!

Jeremiah chap 17 verse 9 "The human heart is the most deceitful of all things, and desperately wicked. Who really knows how bad it is? Our hearts can be the worst enemy of ourselves, self-deception is more frightening than Satan's deception. What do you mean you say, well you can be resurrected out of satanic holds, but when you're in your own denial it's very difficult cause your blind believing in your own conscious or cauterized inception about what you believe. Satan himself does not even want to attack you because you have deceived yourself, just as he thought he can be bigger than the Most High! The point of it all Yeshuah has come through his Holy Spirit leaving us his spirit through this passage, Colossians 1:26 (6 the mystery that has been kept hidden for ages and generations, but is now disclosed to the Lord's people. 27 To them God has chosen to make known among the Gentiles the glorious riches of this mystery, which is Christ in you, the hope of glory. Meaning the prophetic movement that has been preached for the last 1oo years has not been really the true divine correct interpretation.

It has been polluted with hogwash counterfeit doctrine. Many believers have been blinded by these illusions and d illusions of malfunctioning practice, rejecting the Holy Spirit! Read 1 Corinthians 2:16 (Only the perfected (Mature) can understand things of the Spirit! We can come to full complete Maturity. In the situation where Apostle

Peter speaks to Jesus Christ! Matthew 16:4 a wicked and morally unfaithful generation craves a sign, but no sign shall be given to it except the sign of *the prophet* Jonah. Then He left them and went away. The father speaks the divine word of knowledge and understanding of the correct interpretation of the parables in mystery secrets of revelations. Then Yeshua says (6 Jesus said to them, be careful *and* on your guard against the leaven (ferment) of the Pharisees and Sadducee s. The poisoned manna of bread, the false doctrine of theology of tainted dog vomit of his word incorrectly being spewed out to the hearers. Meaning pronounced and announced incorrectly if his divine word. (11 How is it that you fail to understand that I was not talking to you about bread? But beware of the leaven (ferment) of the Pharisees and Sadducee s.12 then they discerned that He did not tell them to beware of the leaven of bread, but of the teaching of the Pharisees and Sadducee s.

Then Yeshua continues to give out divine instructions of understanding (19 I will give you the keys of the kingdom of heaven; and whatever you bind (declare to be improper and unlawful) on earth [I]must be what is already bound in heaven; and whatever you lose (declare lawful) on earth [j]must be what is already loosed in heaven. He is stating for you to come to complete Dominion of authority over the whole earth! 20 Then He sternly *and* strictly charged *and* warned the disciples to tell no one that He was *Jesus* the Christ.21 From that time forth Jesus began [clearly] to show His disciples that He must go to Jerusalem and suffer many things at the hands of the elders and the high priests and scribes, and be killed, and on the third day be raised [k]from death.22 Then Peter took Him aside [l]to speak to Him privately and began to reprove and [m]charge Him sharply, saying, God forbid, Lord! This must never happen to you! 23 But Jesus turned [n]away from Peter and said to him, Get behind Me, Satan! You are in my way [an offense and a hindrance and a snare to me]; for you are [o]minding what partakes not of the nature *and* quality of God, but of men.

Peter was announcing to Yeshua things of his carnal mentality and still could not perceive the divine instructions of the will of his Father in Heaven Yah! Yeshua meant if you cannot understand the true correct teachings of my word you are working for Satan and said get thee behind me Satan! You are an offense and hindrance and a snare to me (Trap, bondage, occult thinking, false doctrine, Paganism, child of Lucifer). In the book of the Bible it speaks of the ten Virgins, that doesn't just mean your clean it means you never had intercourse! Yeshau says the seed is his word (Greek means Sperm). Which means you never been impregnated by the True correct living word of Yahweh if your still a virgin! If we are not going to be impregnated by his word that means your righteousness are nothing but filthy rags (Menstrual cloth). In the next move of Eyeh Asher Eyeh he is saying you better get impregnated by my true correct word of revelation and give birth to my true nature!

Matthew 25 1:13, The bible speaks of the ten virgins, five wise and five foolish, the foolish ones asked the wise give us some of your oil, the wise said no go and buy your oil from the merchants (saying the religious wants something given to them, but the righteous is saying you need to pay a price for it). Doesn't the bible speak carry your cross daily and follow me and take heed to my example! You notice in this passage it speaks of the wise and foolish, the foolish had the door shut in on them, meaning if you do not get into the next move of Yah of God in your life Woe is you! You're all called to become a Prophetic Apostolic Sons of God in his likeness you do not belong to yourselves no matter how good of a person you are. Notice this passage (5 while the bridegroom lingered *and* was slow in coming, they all began nodding their heads, and they fell asleep.6 but at midnight there was a shout, Behold, the bridegroom! Go out to meet him!

In this passage it says they all began to nod their heads and fall asleep even the wise, when the Bridegroom came in slowly, there were others Virgins that were awake in Spirit! The Awakening of this shout knew he was here, there are those virgins who were foolish and did not get impregnated by his word, then there are those virgins who were impregnated but did not give birth to the Full Apostolic move in them that God has for them (OK you might be a little confused, are they not those who are leaders or even sons moving in their gifts and talents but have not come to the full Maturity of his divine nature). These are those virgins who are already birthed and continue to birth and walking the fullness of their divine walk, calling and commission of complete Maturity!

Listen Carefully Matthew 23:27 Woe to you, scribes and Pharisees, pretenders (hypocrites)! For you are like tombs that have been whitewashed, which look beautiful on the outside but inside are full of dead men's bones and everything impure.28 Just so, you also outwardly seem to people to be just *and* upright but inside you are full of pretense and lawlessness *and* iniquity.29 Woe to you, scribes and Pharisees, pretenders (hypocrites)! For you build tombs for the prophets and decorate the monuments of the righteous,30 Saying, If we had lived in the days of our forefathers, we would not have aided them in shedding the blood of the prophets.31 Thus you are testifying against yourselves that you are the descendants of those who murdered the prophets.32 Fill up, then, the measure of your fathers' sins to the brim [so [k]that nothing may be wanting to a full measure].33 You serpents! You spawn of vipers! How can you escape the [l]penalty to be suffered in hell (Gehenna)? Tombs need to be Resurrected also, Resurrected doesn't mean you're going to be raptured to fly away, it also means you Need reestablishment Spiritual truth! The correct way of instructions and teachings of the way you have been taught!

Let me help you a little Saints Ephesians 2; 12 [Remember] that you were at that time separated (living apart) from Christ [excluded from all part in Him], utterly estranged *and* outlawed from the rights of Israel as a nation, and strangers with no share in the sacred compacts of the [Messianic] promise [with no knowledge of or right in God's agreements, His covenants]. And you had no hope (no promise); you were in the world without God.

13 But now in Christ Jesus, you who once were [so] far away, through (by, in) the blood of Christ have been brought near.14 For He is [Himself] our peace (our bond of unity and harmony). He has made us both [Jew and Gentile] one [body], and has broken down (destroyed, abolished) the hostile dividing wall between us,

15 By abolishing in His [own crucified] flesh the enmity [caused by] the Law with its decrees and ordinances [which He annulled]; that He from the two might create in Himself one new man [one new quality of humanity out of

the two], so making peace. 16 And [He designed] to reconcile to God both [Jew and Gentile, united] in a single body by means of His cross, thereby killing the mutual enmity *and* bringing the feud to an end.

17 And He came and preached the glad tidings of peace to you who were afar off and [peace] to those who were near. 18 For it is through Him that we both [whether far off or near] now have an introduction (access) by one [Holy] Spirit to the Father [so that we are able to approach Him]. 19 Therefore you are no longer outsiders (exiles, migrants, and aliens, excluded from the rights of citizens), but you now share citizenship with the saints (God's own people, consecrated and set apart for Himself); and you belong to God's [own] household.

20 You are built upon the foundation of the apostles and prophets with Christ Jesus Himself the chief Cornerstone. 21 In Him the whole structure is joined (bound, welded) together harmoniously, and it continues to rise (grow, increase) into a holy temple in the Lord [a sanctuary dedicated, consecrated, and sacred to the presence of the Lord]. 22 In Him [and in fellowship with one another] you yourselves also are being built up [into this structure] with the rest, to form a fixed abode (dwelling place) of God in (by, through) the Spirit.

It specifically states we were all once estranged, outlawed, also strangers of no hope without any promises of God Yah, with no rights or no Covenants. According to the old covenant to Gods Access to him was the shedding of blood by animals and Tithing. The new Access is brought us near was verse 12 Yeshuas Blood (Contains mystery revelations and secrets), then verse 18 (The Holy Spirit to come Near Him). Yes it states in the word no Man can come unto me but through His only Begotten Son, Yeshua, but Yeshuas also had the Holy Spirit. We need to ask for the Baptism of the Holy Spirit, the edification of speaking in tongues! When Leaders illustrate to you in order to have covenant with God you need to Tithe that is a Demonic Lie! So what they are saying is, so in order to come near to Yah, you need to Tithe ten percent of your money! Where is that in the New Testament or new Covenant!

Let me clarify some more understanding you notice when Moses went to meet Yah at the burning bush, he wanted the people to go to with him to meet him! You notice the people did not go and only Moses. Meaning the people hearts were not totally sold out to him the Father Yah, at one point God told Moses ,OK I will kill and destroy this rotten generation everyone and give you knew people. Moses fell on his face and cried out to the father to spare their lives. So the injunction of well-versed parapsychology or psychological doctrine is stating and telling the people look through me and come through me to get access to the throne of God. The old covenant was the Levite was the access to go into the Holy Holies behind the veil to meet with Eyeh Asher Eyeh and then come out and bless the nation of Israel only not gentiles. So the religious spirit clarifies for you to Exalt me and my foundation of Ministry that God has given me cause, I have special gifts and talents, I am more special and the only way for you to get blessed is through me.

There are several inclusions here people have been manipulated to believe that there Tithe of ten percent is all that is required of them and not there whole heart, because if God had their whole heart that means he owned everything they have not just a percentage! Another one is people have accepted complacency and compromise access point meaning the false religious covering, as long as I pay my tithes and sit or submit under my Pastoral I am covered. Meaning they do not want the Prophetic utterance or apostolic movement of Yahshua in them to become sons of the living god with their talents and gifts and the full maturity of his divine nature within. Another there are some who have accepted the Lucifer spirit of bondage to look through there Pastors and not Yah face to face for themselves. Did not Lucifer manipulate and deceive 1/3 of the angels in heaven to look through him and God himself. How could this take place when the angels are already in the heavenly s of pure bliss! How is it possible to be deceived, special gifts and talents are a dime a dozen but, that means how much more to those who have given and sold there soul to cunning witchery spirits they know not of! How many religions are there, a lot many different ones, how many churches or temples are they in one city, many possibly, preaching and teaching different doctrines for what purpose. How can you be Prophetically Apostolic ally sure you're in the right temple or congregation or around the correct family of people involved in your circle also. Now that can also be a secret or mystery that can be unveiled or never be!

Hebrew 8:8 (8 However, He finds fault with them [showing its inadequacy] when He says, Behold, the days will come, says the Lord, when I will make *and* ratify a new covenant *or* agreement with the house of Israel and with the house of Judah.9 It will not be like the covenant that I made with their forefathers on the day when I grasped them by the hand to help *and* relieve them *and* to lead them out from the land of Egypt, for they did not abide in My agreement with them, and so I withdrew My favor *and* disregarded them, says the Lord.10 For this is the covenant that I will make with the house of Israel after those days, says the Lord: I will imprint My laws upon their minds, even upon their innermost thoughts *and* understanding, and engrave them upon their hearts; and I will be their God, and they shall be My people.11 And it will nevermore be necessary for each one to teach his neighbor and his fellow citizen or each one his brother, saying, Know (perceive, have knowledge of, and get acquainted by experience with) the Lord, for all will know Me, from the smallest to the greatest of them.12 For I will be merciful *and* gracious toward their sins and I will remember their deeds of unrighteousness no more.13 When God speaks of a new [covenant or agreement], He makes the first one obsolete (out of use). And what is obsolete (out of use and annulled because of age) is ripe for disappearance *and* to be dispensed with altogether.

The father Yah speaks of a New better promises of Covenant verse 6(6 But as it now is, He [Christ] has acquired a [priestly] ministry which is as much superior *and* more excellent [than the old] as the covenant (the agreement) of which He is the Mediator (the Arbiter, Agent) is superior *and* more excellent, [because] it is enacted *and* rests upon more important (higher, and nobler) promises.

There are a better new wine of mysteries of interpretation more better promises, the people of old were only a few who can taste and perceive his Dominion ship ,The others there hearts were not in it, the heavenly speaks of Universities of Degrees of Secretes and Mysteries that are unlimited. He wants to give us back our divine nature that was stolen from us since the fall of mankind His dominion to create and recreate!

Really OK lets read the tithe portion of Abraham of what really happened. Genesis 14:17 After his [Abram's] return from the defeat *and* slaying of Chedorlaomer and the kings who were with him, the king of Sodom went out to meet him at the Valley of Shaveh, that is, the King's Valley.18 Melchizedek king of Salem [later called Jerusalem] brought out bread and wine [for their nourishment]; he was the priest of God Most High,19 And he blessed him and said, Blessed (favored with blessings, made blissful, joyful) be Abram by God Most High, Possessor *and* Maker of heaven and earth,20 And blessed, praised, *and* glorified be God Most High, Who has given your foes into your hand! And [Abram] gave him a tenth of all [he had taken].21 and the king of Sodom said to Abram, Give me the persons and keep the goods for yourself. Here is where the carnal mentality comes in with religious doctrine about the tithe. Abraham gave a tenth out of the spoils of war when he defeated the king Chedorlaomer. Abraham never gave a tenth out of his own income what he already had. Notice verse 21 Melchizedek and King of Sodom said keep the good for yourself and give me the people. Melchizedek and King of Sodom rejected the Tithe! So did Abraham really tithe, technically no cause even his heart was in it to tithe it was rejected to become of a new way of a covenant in the future. Melchizedek came to bring communion they had bread and wine! Yeshua says in his word eat of my body and drink my blood and you shall live forever! They had communion back then from the heaven lies. It was a divine instrument of things to come that was given a specific revelation of Jesus Christ (Yeshua dying on the cross).

Let me give you some more Revelation concerning the book of Revelation in its correct context. Revelation 10 verse 1-11.7 But that when the days come when the trumpet call of the seventh angel is about to be sounded, then God's mystery (His secret design, His hidden purpose), as He had announced the glad tidings to His servants the prophets, should be fulfilled (accomplished, completed). The father is speaking to us now he is pouring out his divine intervention of secrets of mysteries that have been hidden. Not the rapture of being taken away to the lord supper table. The marriage feast consists of being impregnated by his word and revelations of secrets and mysteries. That means we are already at the lords table sitting down and eating and feasting through the Holy Spirit not the rapture. Notice verse 9 (So I went up to the angel and asked him to give me the little book. And he said to me, Take it and eat it. It will embitter your stomach, though in your mouth it will be as sweet as honey.

10 So I took the little book from the angel's hand and ate *and* swallowed it; it was as sweet as honey in my mouth, but once I had swallowed it, my stomach was embittered.11 Then they said to me, You are to make a fresh prophecy concerning many peoples *and* races and nations and languages and kings. You are to make a fresh new wine of interpretation of the tongues of fire concerning all mankind afresh in complete dominion ship. We are coming into the complete fulfillment of the marriage feast here and now through prophetic interpretation of his word correctly.

In the book of Revelation 19 verse 6-9 when Yehshua speaks of the supper table The Marriage Supper of the Lamb (6 Then I heard what seemed to be the voice of a great multitude, like the roar of many waters and like the sound of mighty peals of thunder, crying out, "hallelujah! For the Lord our God the Almighty reigns.7 Let us rejoice and exult and give him the glory, for the marriage of the Lamb has come, and his Bride has made herself ready;8 it was granted her to clothe herself with fine linen, bright and pure"—for the fine linen is the righteous deeds of the saints.9 And the angel said[a] to me, "Write this: Blessed are those who are invited to the marriage supper of the Lamb." And he said to me, "These are the true words of God." What he is saying is are you the spirit and can hear the winds of the secrets and mysteries of my new wine in spirit and are you been invited to this feast here and now. Are you bring impregnated and birthing into the new wine and preparing yourself for the marriage in spirit! Remember in the bible Yeshua speaks when I was naked you didn't clothe me. You never allow my Prophetic Apostolic character to be united or birthed within you.

The Book of Revelation of trumpets and shofars are considered the Prophets and them speaking to the body of Christ about the new wine and the next move of God Eyeh Asher Eyeh. He is not talking about the destruction of mankind and the end of age. He is speaking of the Prophets speaking to them about dying to themselves be about dying to self-complete. The Parable means symbolic teachings, the mysteries of secret language of the kingdom hidden in symbolism. The word Unity means when the listener understand and perceive these divine mysteries the parallel comes to a unified state of unity which then comes to a point that's the Sword of truth! The Religious carnal mentality use to think of hearing a trumpet in the air and then we fly away and get a glorified body. No you and me are the trumpets when we trumpet the message the more were coming into redemption of full promise. The bible speaks of pulling your sword out, which is the mysteries and correct understandings of his word. How can you battle when your first of all not in unity with the true Apostle and Prophets speaking of, if not then how can you pull out such a sword of truth. Apostle Peter pulled out his sword and was Rebuked and called Satan! He had the wrong interpretation of what was taught to him and what he understood.

In the bible it speaks of The Apostles saying we need to bring some chairs cause Elijah and Moses is standing right next to you. Yeshua states Elijah has come about future tense but you did not recognize him, speaking of John the Baptist that was beheaded, he was also speaking in future tense the true prophets speaking about these mysteries about bringing back to the Garden of Eden and also back to our glorified body estate! If I said Apocalypse you all would think about the end of the world. In Greek it means Apos means to open, Kolyptos means to open the veils. Every time Yeshua opened up and release revelation there was and Apocalypse taking place opening of the veils of mysteries and parables. It is speaking about revealing in and through us the Son of Glory at the end of this age.

Saints what a beautiful joy ride, let's move on In the book of 2 Thessalonians (1 But relative to the coming of our Lord Jesus Christ (the Messiah) and our gathering together to [meet] Him, we beg you, brethren,

2 Not to allow your minds to be quickly unsettled *or* disturbed or kept excited *or* alarmed, whether it be by some [pretended] revelation of [the] Spirit or by word or by letter [alleged to be] from us, to the effect that the day of the Lord has [already] arrived *and* is here.

3 Let no one deceive *or* beguile you in any way, for that day will not come except the [a]apostasy comes first [unless the predicted great [b]falling away of those who have

professed to be Christians has come], and the man of lawlessness (sin) is revealed, who is the son of doom (of perdition). Now this verse speaks of Apostasy the revelation of the openings of the veils of the true correct teachings of secrets and mysteries and the Christians that think they knew the truth that continue to deny the these teachings. Apostasy to renounce the true divine state what was called and implemented for us they rejected the truth of correct doctrine.

4 Who opposes and exalts himself so proudly *and* insolently against *and* over all that is called God or that is worshiped, [even to his actually] taking his seat in the temple of God, proclaiming that he himself is God. Speaking of those that had not completely died to self.

5 Do you not recollect that when I was still with you, I told you these things?

6 And now you know what is restraining him [from being revealed at this time]; it is so that he may be manifested (revealed) in his own [appointed] time.

7 For the mystery of lawlessness (that hidden principle of rebellion against constituted authority) is already at work in the world, [but it is] restrained only until [c]he who restrains is taken out of the way.

8 And then the lawless one (the antichrist) will be revealed and the Lord Jesus will slay him with the breath of His mouth and bring him to an end by His appearing at His coming. The antichrist is those who oppose the true teachings and still maintain their carnal mentality and also who did not die to themselves completely.

9 The coming [of the lawless one, the antichrist] is through the activity *and* working of Satan and will be attended by

great power and with all sorts of [pretended] miracles and signs *and* delusive marvels—[all of them] lying wonders—

10 And by unlimited seduction to evil *and* with all wicked deception for those who are perishing (going to perdition) because they did not welcome the Truth *but* refused to love it that they might be saved. They did not love the truth, the true correct interpretation of his word they rejected it.

11 Therefore God sends upon them a misleading influence, a working of error *and* a strong delusion to make them believe what is false, the father allows them and sends them a deluded word of false doctrine and allows them to be deceived.

12 In order that all may be judged *and* condemned who did not believe in [who refused to adhere to, trust in, and rely on] the Truth, but [instead] took pleasure in unrighteousness.

Let me give you some more insight on the tabernacle of the outer court, inner court and Holy holies. The outer court of its dimension are 1500 cubits, meaning 1500 hundred years when Moses received the torah from the mountain. The holy place which measurements is 10x20x10 which equals 2000 years until now, describing the body of Christ the church. Now some of you are questioning the rapture of the thousand year rain with Christ. The holy of holies measurements are 10x10x10 of the tabernacle that equals 1,000 we are entering the new millennium of the thousand years reign of our glorified state just like the Garden of Eden. We are entering the glory, were going to be baptized into a new fire of his Shekinah glory that means physically also. This is a mystery not the rapture of being taken away but resurrected into newness of a correct understanding. When Yeshua says prepare for the supper means die to yourselves to receive this newness of life. In order for me to give you complete dominion of Supreme ship you must come to the end of yourselves.

There has been interpretation of faith that is sourly misguided. The definition of faith has another interpretation of revelation, in Hebrew resh means your head, what also in Hebrew means a mountain your head is a mountain, your mind is a mountain. You were made from the dust of earth, your head comes out which your mountain which means high estate your thoughts and understanding. The scripture states if you have faith as small as a mustard seed, you would say to this mountain be thee removed and it would go! If you receive a revelation, that's what the seed meant (Sperm the word of God, the seed Christ is Yeshua), you would say to this mountain the carnal way of thinking be thou removed Yahweh will remove it, because mindsets cause dysfunctions, barriers, blockages and misinterpretations.

ANTHONY MONTOYA

CHAPTER 4

In the book of the bible it speaks of Yeshua dying on the cross, also in some chapters it states he was crucified on a tree, the tree is a symbolic essence of the tree of life. The cross is the symbolic meaning of dying to ourselves coming to the end of self. Yeshua never died when he took his last breath and his breath gave out, in the Greek and Hebrew he breathed one last breath and was reborn, he breathed upon us to receive his divine nature within us. He specifically state when I die I leave you my spirit, Holy Spirit! The tree signifies the tree of life!

Revelation 1:20 20 As for the mystery of the seven stars that you saw in my right hand, and the seven golden lamp stands, the seven stars are the angels of the seven churches, and the seven lamp stands are the seven churches. The mystery is the way he governs his righteousness, the menorah has seven candles, which is in his right hand. He is trying to speak to us through his Holy Spirit, are you and can you really understand the spirit of prophecy, or are you going to be like the Pharisees believing in false teachings. The outer court is the way, inner court or the truth, or the holy of holies the life. The outer court is the thirty fold, inner court sixty fold, Holy of Holies is the 1oo hundred fold realm. What realm are you in, outer court is the babies which is milk, inner court is bread show bread, and the meat is the mystery of secrets hidden manna of the Father. Overcome food Conquer ship Mode Prophets food! Now have you or some of you have heard the interpretations of counterfeit witchery, when the offering is prayed over (O father may it multiply 30, 60,100 hundred fold return talking about money). Here is another one they manipulate in scripture, when you tithe if you get back 3o percent it still prosperous and then etc. 60, 100 fold. Yahweh is not speaking about money at all.

Now some Oxy morons children of Satan speak about the tree of life was the Ten percent, that was there tithe not to touch because if belongs to God! They speak of this that's it's considered the tithe even way back unto Adam and Eve. Wow such hocus pocus interpretation, now let's consider Yahweh said do not touch this tree, the father was only asking for Obedience. The tree of knowledge the forbidden fruit had no evil in it at all. It was through the acts of disobedience which evil was entered in. You notice when eve bit the apple nothing happened. You notice when Adam bit the apple Yahweh said where you are! Now what significance does this mean, Yah Daddy knows everything and knew where he was. The Revelation of it all is he was asking Adam metaphorically where you are, you're not walking in your Dominion ship mode anymore of the spirit. When you obey his divine instructions you're walking in Dominion ship Conquer ship mode, when you eat of the true Prophets food and the correct teachings you succeed in all things. Meditating on his word day and night dying to self completely.

Genesis 1:26 gives us precise interpretation of Dominion ship, 26 God said, Let Us [Father, Son, and Holy Spirit] make mankind in Our image, after Our likeness, and let them have complete authority over the fish of the sea, the birds of the air, the [tame] beasts, and over all of the earth, and over everything that creeps upon the earth. The revelation of this is God created the spirit man, many of us do nothing to feed the spirit man and only concentrate on our fleshly lustful desires that were are controlled by. You notice in Genesis 2:7 Then the Lord God formed man from the [a]dust of the ground and breathed into his nostrils the breath *or* spirit of life, and man became a living being. Yahweh created earthly nature of man the natural glorified body. He gave dominion to the spirit man, so why is everyone fighting things in the flesh while it can only be done by the spirit! The answer is through prayer and worship daily and dying to self-daily.

The Man (Yeshua) felt compassion for the multitudes, but as God the spirit man feed the 5,000 with two fishes and five loaves of bread. As a Man (Yeshua) fell asleep on the boat, as God the spirit man woke up and pointed to the storm peace be still Conquering and disassembling the General demon spirit of the city. As a Man (Yeshua cried when Lazarus died) as God the spirit man he went to the cemetery and said Lazarus get up! As a man (Yeshua) died on the cross as God the spirit man died and rose back up himself!

You notice in the Garden of Eden Satan just didn't want to talk he wanted to plant a seed within her. Seed was at one point in time just a word. Really OK let's clarify this, when eve bit the apple nothing happened. When Adam bit the apple he lost his dominion, when a Husband gives his wife full control over the house and she is not girded underneath the man he loses his dominion. You notice when Adman and Eve conceived a child they had two sons, one says he was born of the wicked one. Adam can only produce what is of him hello. Seed wasn't just a spoken word How did Yeshua become born it was Angel of God from Yahweh and said you shall conceive a child and call him Yeshua, a spoken word. What kind of words are you all talking about, are you speaking life to your children, your bills, lifestyle circumstances, we need to change are language of thinking and talking.

Paul the Apostle wrote 2/3 of the New Testament and speaks of a different season and age at hand. The Apostle Paul and John were speaking of There times and John the revelator was speaking of things that happened after the death of the apostles what was to come and happen which did. In order to understand the times that was never pronounced read the book Rapture less by Jonathan Welton. Paul says 1 Corinthians 15:8 (8 and last of all he was seen of me also, as of one born out of due time. Also Paul states Hebrews 6(6 Therefore let us leave the elementary doctrine of Christ and go on to maturity, not laying again a foundation of repentance from dead works and of faith toward God, 2 and of instruction about washings,[a] the laying on of hands, the resurrection of the dead, and eternal judgment. 3 And this we will do if God permits. 4 For it is impossible, in the case of those who have once been enlightened, who have tasted the heavenly gift, and have shared in the Holy Spirit, 5 and have tasted the goodness of the word of God and the powers of the age to come, 6 and then have fallen away, to restore them again to repentance, since they are crucifying once again the Son of God to their own harm and holding him up to contempt. 7 For land that has drunk the rain that often falls on it, and produces a crop useful to those for whose sake it is cultivated, receives a blessing from God. 8 But if it bears thorns and thistles, it is worthless and near to being cursed, and its end is to be burned.

Let's move on means Divorce in Greek, and the word elementary teaching means logos, So what Paul is saying lets divorce the logos to move on to perfection. Those who have tasted the age to come, there is another age coming future tense, age means world. We are transitioning into a new world than what the Apostle Paul was teaching. Paul stated I am born out of season, I am born at the wrong time, why would Paul say this, he was saying I wanted to be born now here in our time to see the greater works of Yahweh Kingdom transition here and now of what is about to happen.

Let's move on Saints to more Revelation and secrets of Yahweh mysteries. Deuteronomy 29 1:6 These are the words of the covenant, which the LORD commanded Moses to make with the children of Israel in the land of Moab, beside the covenant which he made with them in Horeb.2 And Moses called unto all Israel, and said unto them, Ye have seen all that the LORD did before your eyes in the land of Egypt unto Pharaoh, and unto all his servants, and unto all his land;3 The great temptations which thine eyes have seen, the signs, and those great miracles:4 Yet the LORD hath not given you an heart to perceive, and eyes to see, and ears to hear, unto this day.5 And I have led you forty years in the wilderness: your clothes are not waxen old upon you, and thy shoe is not waxen old upon thy foot.6 Ye have not eaten bread, neither have ye drunk wine or strong drink: that ye might know that I am the LORD your God.

Remember Saints every word has its own meaning character and functions, yet means Moses was grieved in heart about the people not wanting to perceive or understand even though they saw great miracles signs and wonders. Egypt means to be double minded, Pharaoh means to have a double tongue it's a spirit name also. People who speak two tongues, they speak spirit and even they speak lies, there Babylonians ones who are not transparent. Mystery of Babylon Revelation 17:5 and upon her forehead *was* a name written, MYSTERY, BABYLON THE GREAT, and THE MOTHER OF HARLOTS AND

ABOMINATIONS OF THE EARTH. Babylon means mixture in the Anointing, even means mixture in their confusion and speech of their doctrine. People who don't understand what their preaching.

Saints the explanation of this interpretation is for a pure understanding and spirit and in truth. In the Book of Isaiah 61:8 (In the year that king Uzziah died I saw also the LORD sitting upon a throne, high and lifted up, and his train filled the temple.2 Above it stood the seraphim's: each one had six wings; with twain he covered his face, and with twain he covered his feet, and with twain he did fly. The father is raising up seraphim and cherubim army's. 3 And one cried unto another, and said, Holy, holy, holy, is the LORD of hosts: the whole earth is full of his glory.4 and the posts of the door moved at the voice of him that cried, and the house was filled with smoke. The voice of Yahweh his utterance brings deliverance.5 Then said I, Woe is me! For I am undone; because I am a man of unclean lips, and I dwell in the midst of a people of unclean lips: for mine eyes have seen the King, the LORD of hosts. 6 Then flew one of the seraphim's unto me, having a live coal in his hand, which he had taken with the tongs from off the altar:7 And he laid it upon my mouth, and said, Lo, this hath touched thy lips; and thine iniquity is taken away, and thy sin purged. Iniquity means twisted teaching, repent means turn around to untwist yourself. Get the false teachings out of you. 8 Also I heard the voice of the Lord, saying, whom shall I send, and who will go for us? Then said I, Here am I; send me.

The bible speaks of those standing before him you worker of Iniquity I never knew also, means you teacher of lawlessness your twisted teachings. We all can be moving in your gifts and talents of the spirit of grace that's upon you but have no revelation knowledge and no understanding of his true torah his word. The veil upon the Holy of Holies is the picture of the Cherubim with two Flaming swords. Where is that in the bible the Garden of Eden? We are going back into the Garden of Eden the Shekinah Glory of his Presence through us.

Genesis 3: 24 So he drove out the man; and he placed at the east of the garden of Eden Cherubim, and a flaming sword which turned every way, to keep the way of the tree of life. Flaming Sword is the veiled secrets through mysteries of his word prophetic secrets of teachings. Lamed picture Hebrew means teaching Authority in the teaching. Yeshua says take my yoke meaning take on my teaching and learn of me. It also means to put on in ox. Nicodemus ask Jesus Christ what I must do to be born again. John 3 verse 4Nicodemus saith unto him, how can a man be born when he is old? can he enter the second time into his mother's womb, and be born?5Jesus answered, Verily, verily, I say unto thee, Except a man be born of water and of the Spirit, he cannot enter into the kingdom of God.6That which is born of the flesh is flesh; and that which is born of the Spirit is spirit. We must understand his teaching, except the baptism of the Holy Spirit of the edification of speaking in tongues which is water and virtue, Godly character and also prayer life & worship! Psalms 37:7 Thou *art* my hiding place; thou shalt preserve me from trouble; thou shalt compass me about with songs of deliverance. Selah.

There is an announcement of the Mark of the beast thing going around also which I explained in my Second Book the Fruits of Favor and Increase! I explained in detail what was the Mark of the Beast, I explained the mark was a title code in the law book Title 42 666 the SSN card, you're not allowed to buy and sell food. Then I explained also the Mark of the Beast was the carnal mentality and also the prostituting of one another using each other for the gifts and talents. Selling each other like meat for private gain and prostituting each other's personality and character functions for self-gain. Some of you are all scared about the receiving of a computer chip put inside you! OK really the Father is saying what is inscribed in your heart, mind, body and soul, are you sold out for Yahweh! No OK the bible says Ecclesiastes 3:18 I said in mine heart concerning the estate of the sons of men that God might manifest them, and that they might see that they themselves are beasts.

19 For that which befalleth the sons of men befalleth beasts; even one thing befalleth them: as the one dieth, so dieth the other; yea, they have all one breath; so that a man hath no preeminence above a beast: for all is vanity.

20 All go unto one place; all are of the dust, and all turn to dust again.

21 Who knoweth the spirit of man that goeth upward, and the spirit of the beast that goeth downward to the earth? Whoever has the Beastly carnal nature and the spirit of the beast also, the deceitful, lying, cunning, the motive and intentions of their hearts twisted with polluted false doctrine shall return to the dust of the earth!

22 Wherefore I perceive that there is nothing better, than that a man should rejoice in his own works; for that is his portion: for who shall bring him to see what shall be after him?

The Mark means also to be inscribed, what is inscribed within you and all of you totally! In the Old Testament of the bible the lambs were to be sacrificed. What would they do they would chop off their heads first. Who are the lambs in New Testament we are, the bible says my sheep hear my voice, the significance of this is for our heads to be removed to have the mind of Christ. Yeshua says I will send you as martyrs as witnesses unto Judea, sum aria etc. Meaning I will send you with your heads removed for the slaughter to have the mind of Christ only, not your carnal false doctrine mentality. Also another revelation when they would chop off the lambs head they would choke the lamb so the lamb could not squeal or make a noise.

This significance means when you go through trials and tribulations and your being sacrificed you're not supposed to buck and kick, murmur or complain. They did this to me, they did that to me, gossiping, telling God what to do and how he should punish them etc. Get back to the Hebrew understandings. Get off the flesh, Western Greek pagan understandings, repent signifies, if I'm being judged by my time frame and I'm walking forward I'm walking into my future correct, western Greek mindset.

If I'm walking what's being me my past correct again western Greek pagan mindset. Hebrew mindset is totally reversed and exactly opposite, where you're going forward is where you been because you can see it, what you see behind you is your future because you can't see it. Turn around and repent, you turn back to the things you don't know or never seen, you go back to the hidden things.

Isaiah 45:3 And I will give thee the treasures of darkness, and hidden riches of secret places, that thou mayest know that I, the LORD, which call *thee* by thy name, *am* the God of Israel.

You know who wrote the Greek language, Phoenicians and Egyptians, Phoenicians were the descendants of Cain who were the son of ham because he disobeyed and dishonored his father, they were considered accursed people. He went to place called Mount her none is where the Nephilim came down the fallen angels. The Mayans were in contact with the Phoenicians and Canaanites, and the falling angels of Nephilim's. Let me give you another Revelation concerning what I speak of Saints. Did you know the Mayans created the season calendar seasons, months, days and years? They worship the Sun God!

Matthew 24:3 While He was seated on the Mount of Olives, the disciples came to Him privately and said, Tell us, when will this take place, and what will be the sign of Your coming and of the end (the completion, the consummation) of the age? 4 Jesus answered them, be careful that no one misleads you [deceiving you and leading you into error]. False Prophets, teachers and leaders of pagan false doctrine, the Pharisees and Sadducee.

5 For many will come in (on the strength of) my name [[b]appropriating the name which belongs to me], saying, I am the Christ (the Messiah), and they will lead many astray. Using the name of Jesus Christ with many Psychological paraphrases.

6 And you will hear of wars and rumors of wars; see that you are not frightened *or* troubled, for this must take place, but the end is not yet.7 For nation will rise against nation, and kingdom against kingdom, and there will be famines and earthquakes in place after place;8 All this is but the beginning [the early pains] of the [c]birth pangs [of the [d]intolerable anguish]. The dying to self and coming to the end of our self.

9 Then they will hand you over to suffer affliction *and* tribulation and put you to death, and you will be hated by all nations for my name's sake. Are we not all hated by making already since time began?

10 And then many will be offended *and* repelled *and* will [e]begin to distrust *and* desert [Him Whom they ought to trust and obey] *and* will stumble and fall away and betray one another *and* pursue one another with hatred. Isn't the body of Christ some or many already using one another for self-gain and betraying one another, selling each other for profit and private gain?

11 And many false prophets will rise up and deceive *and* lead many into error. Impregnating you with fear and the rapture lawlessness, receiving the mark of the beast the chip and other Mind warfare carnality functions. Religious spirit, keeps you in bondage, low self-esteem, unworthy, no confidence, attacking your immune system. Not allowing you to grow into the Apostolic Prophetic call in everyone's life maturely. Keeping you under control submitting under my fortress, for profit and money, lavishing on your charity of giving.

12 And the love of [f]the great body of people will grow cold because of the multiplied lawlessness *and* iniquity, (False teachings being impregnated in your spirits). 13 But he who endures to the end will be saved. You notice it stated those will be saved. Next verse in this chapter of Matthew, states verse 37 As were the days of Noah, so will be the coming of the Son of Man.38 For just as in those days before the flood they were eating and drinking, [men] marrying and [women] being given in marriage, until the [very] day when Noah went into the ark,39 And they did not know *or* understand until the flood came and swept them all away—so will be the coming of the Son of

Man.40 At that time two men will be in the field; one will be taken and one will be left.41 Two women will be grinding at the hand mill; one will be taken and one will be left.

Saints as the days of Noah who was taken away and taken out the wicked. Noah's family survived, the great tribulation flood. So who is the them and they the Nephilim's and the wicked, they did not know or understand. This is the rapture he is speaking of, we are coming into a new transitional age of God's Kingdom, the millennium the thousand year reign here on earth. Certain ones will not be allowed into the Promise land here on earth, the new transitional age of Yah's Glory. Noah survived and prospered living on to a new earth a new transitional age. The thousand year reign is coming here and now in our time here on earth, were not going anywhere for those who have come to the end of themselves. Mount Hermon in the longitude north of the equator or east is 33.33 degrees in the peris meridian. According the ancients 33 means you have come to reach the highest understanding and teachings. When Yeshua ascended he was 33 years old he achieved perfect wisdom. You notice in the Freemasons lodge the highest form of achievement is 33 degree badge. We're not masons though we serve Yeshua and Yah and the Holy Spirit. Jeremiah 33:3 Call to Me and I will answer you and show you great and mighty things, fenced in and hidden, which you do not know (do not distinguish and recognize, have knowledge of and understand). In other bibles states (I will even show thee great and mighty things hidden secrets and mysteries of ancient old times!). Wow halleluyah saints, give the father some worship and dance before him with all exhaustion of strength.

Remember we spoke every word speaks of characters and functions, Genesis 5 the lineage of the Promised Messiah. Adam-man, Seth-Appoint (set in place), Enoch-mortal (man is mortal), Kenan-sorrow (place to nest), Mahalalel-The blessed father (Praise that illuminates others), Jared-Come up, Enoch-Teaching (Dedicate mysteries), -His death brings, Lamech- The despairing, Noah-Rest. Mans appointed mortal sorrow, the blessed Yahweh will bring down, Teaching and dedication principles and mystery revelations, bringing his death resurrecting and bringing the despairing rest! What a beautiful father we serve to understand how he knew before time how everything was going to work out.

You have four elements of clothing according the Robe of the Rabbis in the Old Testament, One you had the Badgers skin (Which is the Mark of the Beast your carnal mentality). Then you have Rams skin which what the red cloth his atoning blood covering us, the lamb within you which is Christ. Curtain goat hair (Which is the sin offering of the curtain). Fourth you have the fine linen the high priest wore a robe of fine linen. The book of Revelation states, the bride is wearing a garment of fine linen which is the righteous acts of the Saints. Righteous also means broken down right correct understanding, when you have a correct understanding which covers you with his word through the Holy Spirit which makes you the bride of Christ. Ephesians 3:10 [The purpose is] that through the church the [c]complicated, many-sided wisdom of God in all its infinite variety *and* innumerable aspects might now be made known to the angelic rulers and authorities (principalities and powers) in the heavenly sphere. The inner layer had many colors, manifold means multi-color and character might be known to the church. When we are preaching to the church the mysteries and secrets of the kingdom that they we are the true sons of Yahweh.

Paul the Apostle was fighting what? Some of you are still confused about the Apocalypse or Mark of the Beast computer chip, how retarded, 1 Corinthians 15:31 I protest by your rejoicing which I have in Christ Jesus our Lord, I die daily. 32 If after the manner of men I have fought with beasts at Ephesus, what advantageth it me, if the dead rise not? Let us eat and drink; for tomorrow we die. He was coming against the beastly mentality of carnal Christians that's what he was fighting. When he writes his name on you, you walk and act like him and become like him. The fulfillment back to the garden of Eden, where Adam was created, what was lost in the book of revelation, will be restored how it once was in your natural divine state full Dominion! We're not running from the Antichrist, I'm running after the antichrist, the antichrist in my mind, Christ means anointing, anointing means teaching, the Holy Spirit is the teacher. Anyone against the teaching of the true teachings are antichrist. He is going to put you in tribulation and puts pressure on you to get all the carnal teachings out of you, burning out all the wrong character out of you, coming out of yourself.

False prophets come to establish your carnal mindsets, talking about you, your tithing opens up the heavens and the Hand of Eyeh Asher Eyeh, Car, House, Prosperity. Teaching you to seek his hand and not His face, and his character, of life. Saints here is another verse from the bible which I speak of, Psalms 73:20 As a dream when *one* awaketh; *so*, O Lord, when thou awakest, thou shalt despise their image.21 Thus my heart was grieved, and I was pricked in my reins.22 So foolish *was* I, and ignorant: I was *as* a beast before thee. Paul the Apostle was once a

Beast, Pharisee until he got knocked off his horse on his way to Damascus. Then he had to go where to the Wilderness to die to self completely, for about three years in the wilderness he had the Holy Spirit burn out all of the Torah teachings his was raised from. Paul 14 years of age according to Rabbi's, he had the torah memorized. It needed to be all burned out. You notice in the Picture of the Last Supper where John's head was and ear, it was on Yeshuas heart. Paul could hear the secret mysteries of the torah inscribed in Yeshuas heart. Doesn't it say in his word I will inscribe my torah in their hearts and minds? You can hear my heart that's why he allowed him to write the book of Revelations.

It states in his word about the Pearly gates of heaven, 12,000 cubits, its foundation the gates has 12 doorways, times that equals 144,000 thousand. Why the number 12, only the Apostolic Company will be allowed into the pearly gates, pearls means revelation of his true word and character inscribed in their hearts. The book of Ephesians 3 states these hidden mysteries are coming only from the Apostles and Prophets.

You notice in the bible when Yeshua feed the five thousand souls, with two fish and two loaves of bread, He stated eat of my flesh and drink of my blood. They all left him and weeded out only those who wanted to hear with a true repentant heart. It only became 12 out of 5,000 souls. In the book Acts the upper room there was 500 that began, 50 means jubilee x10 means the law, only 120 were left to receive the Baptism of the tongues of fire! You notice in the bible as the days of Noah it took him 120 years to build the Ark of covenant. You notice when Yeshua tells them to stay and they end up leaving what happened, when you die you end up in hell.

There was 380 that left, the number 380 means going back to bondage slavery and death.

Saints remember when they had to put the lamb's blood on their doorposts, to be saved from the angel of death, this was in the times of Moses. What's the doorpost your forehead, John tells us Yah is light and if we walk in the light as his son is in the light there is no darkness, then the blood of Yeshua cleanses us of our sins. The light is the revelation of his teachings and understandings. The doorpost is also your heart a gateway to his heart! Oh really Saints some of you are probably wondering what is the truth to all this. Well Most congregations have no clue what deliverance is or the move of the Holy Spirit is, then why are you attending there. Many Saints go to big revivals and hear a big message preached with big loud boastful words with no Deliverance or inner healing of the gifts of the Holy Spirit taken place at all.

In the Book of Genesis he created what on the fourth day, the son, the moon and the stars. What was the father speaking of from that point he stated I am bringing my son Yeshua on the 4th day. Its only 2,000 years since the cross, didn't I state were walking into a new age of transition of a kingdom. The new millennium 1,000 year reign with Christ in full dominion. Let me clarify this to you some more, **1 Corinthians 15:39-41 (KJV)**

39 All flesh is not the same flesh: but there is one kind of flesh of men, another flesh of beasts, another of fishes, and another of birds. **40** There are also celestial bodies, and bodies terrestrial: but the glory of the celestial is one, and the glory of the terrestrial is another. **41** There is one glory of the sun, and another glory of the moon, and another glory of the stars: for one star differ from another star in glory. Doesn't it state in the bible he is the Son of

Glory Yeshua, He is the Bright and morning Star, He is also the Moon glory because around the circle or circumference of the moon all the feasts happen. The 7th day is what when he rested, he is talking about his army walking in the fullness of Glory.

In the book of the bible Yeshua says, Matthew 24:44 The Lord said to My Lord, Sit at My right hand until I put your enemies under your feet? Then why in the book of Corinthians why does it look like Paul is Contradicting himself. Everyone has a mentality Christ made all things manifest at the cross 2,000 years ago, so why is Yeshua sitting at the right hand of the father and he is not coming yet. Yet everything was done at the cross he has all power and dominion. We are not walking in that fullness yet, 1 Corinthians 15:24 Then *cometh* the end, when he shall have delivered up the kingdom to God, even the Father; when he shall have put down all rule and all authority and power. 25 For he must reign, till he hath put all enemies under his feet. 26 The last enemy *that* shall be destroyed *is* death. 27 For he hath put all things under his feet. But when he saith all things are put under *him, it is* manifest that he is accepted, which did put all things under him. 28 And when all things shall be subdued unto him, then shall the Son also himself be subject unto him that put all things under him that God may be all in all. This is a Prophetic Mystery, Dominion means what feet, He is Yeshua Head of the Church, and we are his feet. Until we put the enemy under our feet which is Christ within us he will not return for no rapture Saints. That means the whole earth walking and have dominion just like Adam was given full Dominion over the air, fish and sea the whole earth. We are entering into a new glorified body here and now, 1,000 year reign 3rd day, 3000 years. The 4th day is his return after 1,000 years more, he is not coming back for a church that has falling away he is coming back for an overcoming church.

You notice he made the sun, moon, stars, three equality, Father, Son, Holy Spirit, the Tabernacle, outer court, inner court, Holy of Holies. We are entering in the Holy of Holies a new time frame of existence a new world the Promise land Inheritance. The 3rd day, 3000 years. It is barely 2014, that means he is not returning until another 986 years, this explanation is also explained in my second book the fruits of favor and increase! We are entering in back to the Garden of Eden a Glorified immortal body. Isaiah 65:20 20 There shall no more be in it an infant who lives but a few days, or an old man who dies prematurely; for the child shall die a hundred years old, and the sinner who dies when only a hundred years old shall be [thought only a child, cut off because he is] accursed.21 They shall build houses and inhabit them, and they shall plant vineyards and eat the fruit of them.22 They shall not build and another inhabit; they shall not plant and another eat [the fruit]. For as the days of a tree, so shall be the days of my people, and my chosen *and* elect shall long make use of *and* enjoy the work of their hands. How long do trees live Saints from 600-1,000 years rooted in planted firmly fixed.

We were to have Dominion of the birds of the air, beasts of the earth and the fish of the sea, you and I must come into all three dominions. The foul of the air is Satan, the general demon spirits of cites and nations, what is the beast of the earth us the beastly nature, who are the fish of the sea us all humanity, I am going to make you fishers of men.

CHAPTER 5

The Elijah ministries are parables and patterns of mysteries, Elijah went into a village and meet a widow woman, picking wood, hay and stone, wood is symbolic of sin. She lost her husband the Christ (Yeshua) within here, she had a son that was dying, I am going to take some flour and oil, flour is symbolic of the word, the oil is the anointing. We have a little understanding of knowledge of the word and a little anointing left bake a cake and die. Until she met the Prophet, he said u give me what you have, I'm going to make you fast, cause I'm going to eat it, if you receive as a prophet you go into the village and get all the vegetables and the people and fill up this house I will give you the knowledge and fill you up with the spirit of living waters. Ephesians chap 3:3 For this reason [[a]because I preached that you are thus built up together], I, Paul, [am] the prisoner of Jesus the Christ [b]for the sake *and* on behalf of you Gentiles—2 Assuming that you have heard of the stewardship of God's grace (His unmerited favor) that was entrusted to me [to dispense to you] for your benefit,3 [And] that the mystery (secret) was made known to me *and* I was allowed to comprehend it by direct revelation, as I already briefly wrote you.4 When you read this you can understand my insight into the mystery of Christ.5 [This mystery] was never disclosed to human beings in past generations as it has now been revealed to His holy apostles (consecrated messengers) and prophets by the [Holy] Spirit.

If there is no True Apostles and Prophets in your church building what are you doing there, if there is no fivefold ministry in your church what are you doing there. Where does it state in his word, pastors, teachers, evangelists, bishops, deacons, reverend etc. move the vision of the church or the mystery and secrets? Yes we are one body and we all need one another yes, its called unity, but who is in charge saints the Apostles and Prophets. Matthew chap 17:17 And six days after this, Jesus took with Him Peter and James and John his brother, and led them up on a high mountain (Mindset) by themselves, (these three revelators went through a higher state of mindsets).2 And He was transfigured before them; and His face shone as the sun, and His raiment was white as the light.3 And behold, there appeared unto them Moses and Elijah, talking with Him. Transfiguration mean form, metamorphosis means form and nature in Hebrew, when you receive the secrets and mysteries of the kingdom even your physical body of nature transforms into a greater glory! Some may be questioning yourselves, personally on Face book or Myspace five years ago, a prophetess met with a women who went to heaven or hell. She has pictures all over when she prays for people over hundreds of photos you can see the demon spirits in each photo very clear, hundreds of different spirits all over people. Also she was 78 eight years old, here body and face shows the significance she looks like she's 33years of age to the tee. My prophet's friend spoke with her personally and she stated men of 20 to 30 years of age are always asking her out even asking her to marry.

It is 2014, Methuselah live 969 years, and if you add 14 years to 969 it comes bout to 983 years. A prophet spoke to my mother and stated the father Yah through the Holy Spirit is going to give her instructions concerning the next 14years of her life. If you add 14-17 years it equals 1,000 years. It is possible we have about 14-17 years to before we come into this glorified state of entering in the Garden of Eden. Meaning we have 14-17 years of work to burn out all the iniquity of false teachings of the saints, and the dying to self and coming to the end of self. Some already have entered this state of transition, some might come into it in the next two to three years. Some of us who already have ate off of the table, we need to go into a wilderness of this new wine, just like Paul did for three years! Saints about the time frame I am just putting some opinion on this but you notice the number are equivalent to 7 which means perfection comes and is here and at hand no matter what. Two double Sevens equals 14 also means double portion, three years means process and training ground which if you add 14 plus 3 equals 17 just symbolic meanings. Paul went to the wilderness for three years, the disciples were taught by Yeshua for three years. Matthew 13:15 15 For this people's heart has waxed gross, and their ears are dull of hearing, and their eyes they have closed (secrets and mysteries) of his Hebrew teachings of the word; lest at any time they should see with their eyes, and hear with their ears, and should understand with their heart, and should be converted, and I should heal them (meaning bring them back into their glorified body's back into the Garden of Eden).' 16 But blessed are your eyes, for they see; and your ears, for they hear.17 For verily I say unto you, that many prophets and righteous men have desired to see those things which ye see, and have not seen them, and to hear those things which ye hear, and have not heard them. What's this message symbolic of the hidden secrets and mysteries that is about to be revealed our entering into a new age back to the Garden of Eden it's a Mystery, they desired it but could not see it cause it was not that time of age and season for them. That's why Paul the Apostle stated I am a man born out of Season and time. He saw the future and wanted to be here with us in this new Realm of Glory and transitional age.

Let me explain to you when Leaders Pastors Prophets speaks to you about false teachings about seed, which is your mind, which is the word of Yah and operate under the spiritual of control about sowing your seed of money and Yah is going to bless you, you just entered into a spirit of Witchcraft (the seed is your money) is false not money. Matthew 13:22-25 22 He also that received the seed among the thorns is he that heareth the Word; and the cares of this world and the deceitfulness of riches choke the Word, and he becomes unfruitful.23 But he that received seed into the good ground is he that heareth the Word and understandeth it; who also beareth fruit and bringeth forth, some a hundredfold, some sixty, some thirty."24 Another parable put He forth before them, saying, "The Kingdom of Heaven is likened unto a man who sowed good seed in his field; 25 but while men slept, his enemy came and sowed tares among the wheat, and went his way.

Let's continue verse 26But when the blades had sprung up and brought forth fruit, then appeared the tares (the wicked ones false prophets and teachers) also.27 So the servants of the householder came and said unto him, 'Sir, didst not thou sow good seed in thy field (sowing was the Parables of secrets of mysteries of his word) From whence then hath come the tares?'28 He said unto them, 'An enemy hath done this.' The servants said unto him, 'Wilt thou then have us go and gather them up?'29 But he said, 'Nay, lest while ye gather up the tares, ye root up also the wheat with them.30 Let both grow together until the harvest, and in the time of harvest (it's not the rapture of his coming) I will say to the reapers, "Gather ye together first the tares, and bind them in bundles to burn them, but gather the wheat into my barn."' The tares are the wicked, the father is saying hurry and come into my divine revelation of my word, the wicked are going to be raptured and taking away not we being saved from disaster or end of the world hocus pocus.

Verse 35 that it might be fulfilled which was spoken by the prophet, saying, "I will open my mouth in parables; I will utter things which have been kept secret from the foundation of the world."36 Then Jesus sent the multitude away and went into the house, and His disciples came unto Him, saying, "Explain unto us the parable of the tares of the field."37 He answered and said unto them, "He that soweth the good seed is the Son of Man(righteous ones speaking of secrets and mysteries).38 The field is the world(unrighteous-heart or ministry), the good seed are the children of the Kingdom, but the tares are the children of the wicked one.39 The enemy that sowed them is the devil, the harvest is the end of the world, and the reapers are the angels(Elijah ministries, we are messengers of fire, his angels us) shall cast them into a furnace of fire: there shall be wailing and gnashing of teeth40 As therefore the tares are gathered and burned in the fire, so shall it be at the end of this world.41 The Son of Man shall send forth His angels, and they shall gather out of His Kingdom all things that offend and them that do iniquity,(iniquity also means false teachings wrong doctrine).43 Then shall the righteous shine forth as the sun in the Kingdom of their Father. Who hath ears to hear, let him hear? Doesn't it state in the bible I will send my messengers to prepare the way before me? We are the messengers, it's not speaking about the rapture and end of the world, 666, were are going to be rapture d and taken away by angels sorry wrong religious witchery false doctrine. The wrong interpretation is to keep you bound up in fear and no confidence so you can continue to pay alms and dues with your tithes to the leaders to build there kingdom and lavishing on your charity of giving, the ones who do not speak unto you secrets and mysteries of the kingdom, dying to yourself or coming to the end of yourself! No true Apostles and Prophets in your church building run out of your church as fast as you can.

Saint in the end of age it specifically sates when this new revelation of true doctrine is being preached it will offend them, most congregations have been hearing the same word of doctrine for ages not the ones I'm speaking of in my books. These are hidden secrets mysteries, a new era of teachings, parables are mysteries of the torah of Yah. Once this message begins to come out there is going to be a great falling away from the faith. When it states the wicked will be cast into the fire (they will be destroyed underneath your feet) no power or control or on top anymore.

When Yeshua says to forgive 490 times in one day, you get offended by peoples cell phones going off in the church, talking right next to you, chewing gum in a service any little thing that offends you, your still a baby and have not matured, or they correct you in some kind of way and it offends you, you still need dying to self. Once more Matthew 13; 49 so shall it be at the end of the world: the angels shall come forth and sever the wicked from among the just, 50 and shall cast them into the furnace of fire: there shall be wailing and gnashing of teeth."51 Jesus said unto them, "Have ye understood all these things?" They said unto Him, "Yea, Lord."52 Then said He unto them, "Therefore every scribe who is instructed unto the Kingdom of Heaven is like unto a man that is a householder, who bringeth forth out of his treasure things new and old." Every scribe which is us, teachers or what's being inscribed in your heart, treasures of the Old Testament and New Testament revelation mysteries of the kingdom apostolically and prophetically.

Yeshua even states in his word he want to deliver us all, Yeshua came that not one should perish, Malachi 3:14 Ye have said: 'It is vain to serve God; and what profit is it that we have kept His ordinance, and that we have walked mournfully before the LORD of hosts? 15 So now we call the proud happy; yea, they that work wickedness are set up; yea, they that tempt God are even delivered.'" He even with his love wants to deliver the wicked from themselves.

2 Corinthians 3:12 since we have such [glorious] hope (such joyful and confident expectation), we speak very freely *and* openly *and* fearlessly. Paul the apostle was coming against the whole religious organization of human race. 13 Nor [do we act] like Moses, who put a veil over his face so that the Israelite s might not gaze upon the finish of the vanishing [splendor which had been upon it]. Apocalypse means removal the veils of mysteries and secrets, Yah told Moses since you have this mystery in you and you understand the teachings, cover it up, I'm going to shut the door to the people I'm not going to allow them into the greater glory.

14 In fact, their minds were grown hard *and* calloused [they had become dull and had lost the power of

understanding]; for until this present day, when the Old Testament (the old covenant) is being read, that same veil still lies [on their hearts], not being lifted [to reveal] that in Christ it is made void *and* done away. Means your heart are veiled to the secrets of the Old Testament and New Testament mysteries, heart and doorposts are your minds and hearts. If you don't have the mind of Christ which is the anointing of The Holy Spirit, also the edification of speaking in tongues everything is done away with, meaning your heart and minds are done and buried and dead, nothing but a white washed tomb.

15 Yes, down to this [very] day whenever Moses is read, a veil lies upon their minds *and* hearts.16 But whenever a person turns [in repentance] to the Lord, the veil is stripped off *and* taken away.17 Now the Lord is the Spirit, and where the Spirit of the Lord is, there is liberty (emancipation from bondage, freedom).18 And all of us, as with unveiled face, [because we] continued to behold [in the Word of God] as in a mirror the glory of the Lord, are constantly being transfigured into His *very own* image in ever increasing splendor *and* from one degree of glory to another; [for this comes] from the Lord [Who is] the Spirit.

When your hearts are not hardened from this mysteries and teachings, liberty to receive the revelation and teachings of his true prophetic word. Metamorphosis, a transfiguration own image means a mirror, to look at ourselves in his image, through a process of unveiling revelations.

Romans 12:12 I beseech you therefore, brethren, by the mercies of God, that ye present your bodies a living sacrifice, holy, acceptable unto God, which is your reasonable service.2 And be not conformed to this world, but be ye transformed by the renewing of your mind, that ye may prove what is that good and acceptable and perfect will of God. This is saying not to be conformed to the false teachings of doctrine of this (Age) but be what transformed (Metamorphosis) to be transfigured by the renewing of your mind. Learning new secrets and mysteries of the kingdom by who, His Apostles and Prophets. Hosea 4:6 My people are destroyed for lack of knowledge; because you [the priestly nation] have rejected knowledge, I will also reject you that you shall be no priest to Me; seeing you have forgotten the law of your God, I will also forget your children. Hello the father says I will reject you because you do not want to be raptured into a new pure and correct teachings of his word of secrets and mysteries. We need to all have more grace, mercy and unconditional forgiving love one to another more than ever.

Pastors, bishops, evangelists, teachers, deacons, Reverend are not in charge of the church in any church building. This is Yeshuas word and his teachings. The church is so dead with one hour services to two hours services and the worship only last no more than 3o minutes. Titus 3:4 But when the goodness and loving-kindness of God our Savior to man [as man] appeared, 5 He saved us, not because of any works of righteousness that we had done, but because of His own pity *and* mercy, by [the] cleansing [bath] of the new birth (regeneration) and renewing of the Holy Spirit, 6 Which He poured out [so] richly upon us through Jesus Christ our Savior. Washing means, a new baptism just like the book Acts, when fire came down upon the upper room 120 people of Yah. They received a new revelation of understanding, regeneration means a radical change of mind, in Hebrew and Greek even means a (Genesis) a new spiritual growth, that restoration of the primal perfect condition of things which existed before the fall of our Parents Adam and Eve Hello!. Pouring of the new wine, the book of revelation is speaking of the hidden mysteries of the Old Testament!

There are 4 levels of Wisdom, Pshat simple understanding-Common people, Remez-hinted meaning Noble and Layers, Drush-allegorical-investigation a king searches out the hidden treasures-Kingly, Sod-secret understanding Apostolic, Prophets. Matthew 8:20 And Jesus replied to him, Foxes have holes and the birds of the air have lodging places, but the Son of Man has nowhere to lay His head. What Yeshua was speaking of was he was looking for a body of people to understand the Mind of Christ, people who were mature enough to handle the mind of Christ! Amos 3:7 surely the Lord God will do nothing [a]without revealing His secret to His servants the prophets. Ephesians 3:2 Assuming that you have heard of the stewardship of God's grace (His unmerited favor) that was entrusted to me [to dispense to you] for your benefit,3 [And] that the mystery (secret) was made known to me *and* I was allowed to comprehend it by direct revelation, as I already briefly wrote you.4 When you read this you can understand my insight into the mystery of Christ.5 [This mystery] was never disclosed to human beings in past generations as it has now been revealed to His holy apostles (consecrated messengers) and prophets by the [Holy] Spirit.

Proverbs 15:22 22 Where there is no counsel (Sode means Prophetic revelation of Yah mysteries and secrets), purposes are frustrated, but with many counselors they are accomplished.

Deuteronomy 32:32 "Give ear, O ye heavens, and I will speak; and hear, O earth, the words of my mouth.2 My doctrine shall drop as the rain, my speech shall distill as the dew, as the small rain upon the tender herb, and as the showers upon the grass. This symbolic symbolism's means let my revelation fall like the rain. 1 Kings 18:41 And Elijah said unto Ahab, "Get thee up, eat and drink; for there is a sound of abundance of rain." His Revelation to human race and mankind.

42 So Ahab went up to eat and to drink. And Elijah went up to the top of Carmel; and he cast himself down upon the earth and put his face between his knees,

43 and said to his servant, "Go up now, look toward the sea." And he went up and looked, and said, "There is nothing." And he said, "Go again," seven times.

44 And it came to pass at the seventh time that he said, "Behold, there ariseth a little cloud out of the sea, like a man's hand." And he said, "Go up, say unto Ahab, 'Prepare thy chariot, and get thee down, that the rain stop thee not.'" Cloud symbolic his Presence, sea means in Hebrew absolute certainty, man's hand the Fivefold ministries of Elijah's to come to prepare the way and make the crooked paths straight. Repentance is also revelation of twisted thinking of language.

45 And it came to pass in the meantime, that the heaven was black with clouds and wind, and there was a great rain. And Ahab rode, and went to Jezreel. Cloud means Shekinah Glory his presence, wind means the Holy Spirit, Rain mysteries secrets of the Kingdom.

Leviticus 10:6 6 And Moses said unto Aaron and unto Eleazar and unto Ithamar, his sons, "Uncover not your heads, neither rend your clothes, lest ye die, and lest wrath come upon all the people; but let your brethren, the whole house of Israel, bewail the burning which the LORD hath kindled. If you tear or divide the Holy Spirit or freeze the Holy Spirit, you will put a curse upon you and you will die. Do not tear your garment, meaning do not reject the teaching of the Holy Spirit! Matthew 26:61 and said, "This fellow said, 'I am able to destroy the temple of God and to build it in three days.'" Saints this is 2014, we are entering into the third tabernacle faze, the next 1,ooo year reign, the 3day outpouring of his new wine!. John 2:1-11(And on the third day there was a marriage in Cana of Galilee, and the mother of Jesus was there; The Marriage Feast being Married to his Shekinah Glory becoming one with the Father. You notice verse 10 and said to him, everyone else serves his best wine first, and when people have drunk freely, then he serves that which is not so good; but you have kept back the good wine until now! The father served them some good wine but not the best, he stated but have kept the last new 2nd wine until now!

Matthew 26:62 and the high priest arose and said unto Him, "Answer-est thou nothing? What is it which these witnesses say against thee?" Caiaphas is not a real high priest that why Yeshua stood silent.

63 But Jesus held His peace. And the high priest answered and said unto Him, "I adjure thee by the living God that thou tell us whether thou be the Christ, the Son of God." Caiaphas did not know who Yeshua was, but John did instantly when he saw him, there are those who cannot dis cipher what are the true teaching of the Holy Spirit and Discern False Doctrine.

64 Jesus said unto him, "Thou hast said; nevertheless I say unto you, hereafter shall ye see the Son of Man sitting at the right hand of Power, and coming in the clouds of heaven."65 Then the high priest rent his clothes, saying,

"He hath spoken blasphemy! What further need have we of witnesses? Behold, now ye have heard his blasphemy!

Revelation 9:11 and they had a king over them, the angel of the bottomless pit, whose name in the Hebrew tongue is Abaddon, but in the Greek tongue his name is Apollyon. Apollyon means to tear or break off a branch of fine linen, also brings an army of locusts with him, that eats of Yahweh tree of good fruit. Joel 2;25 "And I will restore to you the years that the locust hath eaten, the canker worm and the caterpillar and the Palmer worm, My great army which I sent among you. When you reject the Holy Spirit the Spirit of Abaddon has access and divine right to eat you up in every way. This army of Locusts also speaks of Yahweh's army, which army are you apart of the spirit of Abaddon which is Apollyon or the Final great army of Elijah ministries. The bottomless pit means no deep things of God no revelation and no secrets, nothing but white washed dead tombs, your nothing but a coffin like in a cemetery. Religious systems are being led by the Principality Spirit of Abaddon.

OK Saints more revelation of what I speak of 1 Corinthians 15:49 And as we have borne the image of the earthy, we shall also bear the image of the heavenly.50 Now this I say, brethren, that flesh and blood cannot inherit the Kingdom of God; neither doth corruption inherit in corruption.51 Behold, I show you a mystery:(Revelation of secrets and mysteries) we shall not all sleep; but we shall all be changed52 in a moment, in the twinkling of an eye, at the last trumpet (Apostles and Prophets). For the trumpet shall sound, and the dead shall be raised incorruptible, and we shall be changed.53 For this corruptible (false doctrine teachings) must put on in corruption, and this mortal must put on immortality.54 So when this corruptible shall have put on in corruption, and this mortal shall have put on immortality, then shall be brought to pass the saying that is written: "Death is swallowed up in victory." When you have false doctrine of twisted mindsets, your considered dead inside no life, when you do not grow up and mature in character and heart transplant of dying to self you're in corruption, in bondage, your considered dead, lifeless. 1 Corinthians 15:42 so also is the resurrection of the dead: It is sown in corruption; it is raised in in corruption. Resurrection means a reestablishing of spiritual truth! Resurrection also means rapture to a new state of understanding, to be caught up to what is at hand!

Revelation (10:7) in contrast, is mans (redemption from all iniquity) and its consequences: a mystery once hidden in God's secret counsels, dimly-shadowed forth in types and prophecies, but now more and more clearly revealed according as the Good news kingdom develops itself up to its fullest consummation. Yah's prophets revealing the secrets and mysteries of the kingdom when it begins to rain revelation like raindrops unlimited, teachings of revelations from Glory to Glory constantly, when we get closer to the kingdom we learn more truth in revelation and it never stops but rains. What does this signify meaning the same boring false doctrine being preached over and over, with no revelations or secrets or mysteries at all, meaning it's not raining yet is it in your church, with no Apostles and Prophets as the leader in the church buildings.

Saints let's move on Revelation 2:17 He who is able to hear, let him listen to *and* heed what the Spirit says to the assemblies (churches). To him who overcomes (conquers)one who crosses over (Hebrew), I will give to eat of the manna (Secrets mysteries)that is hidden, and I will give him a white stone with a new name engraved on the stone, which no one knows *or* understands except he who receives it. White stone is the Ten Commandments which was in the Ark of the Covenant. When the father gives his mysteries and secrets which no one knows or understands except the one who receives it. It just specifically stated this new understandings no one can understand only to the one who receive it. Amos 3:7 surely the Lord God will do nothing [a]without revealing His secret to His servants the prophets.

ANTHONY MONTOYA

CHAPTER 6

Yeshua had a crown of thorns, the thorns means in Hebrew to be hedged in, (He has the Good News within him). So when you die spiritually that means you die to your old carnal way of thinking. He was crucified at Golgotha (Place of Skulls), meaning we need the mind of Christ, he was crucified on his head skull. Exodus 16:8 8 And Moses said, *this shall be*, when the LORD shall give you in the evening flesh to eat (Good news Revelation Secrets and mysteries Yeshua Body) and in the morning bread to the full; for that the LORD hearth your murmurings which ye murmur against him: and what *are* we? your murmurings *are* not against us, but against the LORD.9 And Moses spoke unto Aaron, Say unto all the congregation of the children of Israel, Come near before the LORD: for he hath heard your murmurings.

Bread means in Hebrew Chet lamed Mem, Lamed is Yoke-teaching, take my teachings yoke yourself to me and learn of me. What do you put a yoke on an Ox, Ox means his Apostles, we were created to be Apostolic people. Chet is a (wall), Mem is water that flows, and it saying there is a fight between the teaching and the flow of the spirit. Saints remember every word deals with Character and function.

Bread means flour and water, Anointing means to press in (Teaching), it also means Tribulation, meaning when you fight against it, it must be pushed within you or shoved down your throat to eat it. Doesn't it say Yahweh reigns on the just and unjust? Mountain is also considered your Head, 1Corinthians 10:4 for the weapons of our warfare

are not carnal, but mighty through God for the pulling down of strongholds,

5 casting down imaginations and every high thing that exalted itself against the knowledge of God, and bringing into captivity every thought to the obedience of Christ. You notice verse 5 (Every High thing that exalted itself).

Alright more Saints OK, 1 Corinthians 17:21 17 For this very cause I sent to you Timothy, who is my beloved and trustworthy child in the Lord, who will recall to your minds my methods of proceeding *and* course of conduct *and* way of life in Christ, such as I teach everywhere in each of the churches.18 Some of you have become conceited *and* arrogant *and* pretentious, counting on my not coming to you.19 But I will come to you [and] shortly, if the Lord is willing, and then I will perceive *and* understand not what the talk of these puffed up *and* arrogant spirits amount to, but their force ([d]the moral power and excellence of soul they really possess).20 For the kingdom of God consists of *and* is based on not talk but power ([e]moral power and excellence of soul).21 Now which do you prefer? Shall I come to you with a rod of correction, or with love and in a spirit of gentleness?

Yeshua specifically stated I will recall to your minds your carnal way of thinking of false doctrine, my methods (The orchestration of the leading of the Holy spirit, proceeding (to bring out, to bring forth, the way its announced) Course means (the way its layed out the foundations of speech administered correctly, absolute to stick. The four levels of interpretation I just explained earlier in this book. Conduct means in Hebrew (bring forth, carry, lead forth) the Anointing of his Shekinah Glory how it is carried out strategically with divine instructions, it also means, to be lead out of Captivity (Psalms 45: 10 Hear, O daughter, consider, submit, *and* consent to my instruction: forget also your own people and your father's house; 11 So will the King desire your beauty; because He is your Lord, be submissive *and* reverence *and* honor Him. It states I will perceive and understand not what the talk of these puffed up and arrogant spirits amount to, some of you have diabolical and religious spirits, because of your way of thinking and understanding of the word!. It also states shall I come to you with a Rod of correction (Some bibles say a whip) meaning, with great tribulation to make and force you to drink and eat of me, and also to whip it into you.

Saints do you or have you ever whipped or used the rod of correction on your own kids for their own natural and way understanding and thinking for their own good hello!. Bread in Hebrew also means to overcome, when pizza is made its beaten and mixed together properly, Revelation 2: 26 and he that overcome and keepeth my works unto the end, to him will I give power over the nations. (Word) in Hebrew means a chain of letters to make up a powerful unbreakable truth or covenant, the word sickness in Hebrew means a break in the chain.

So when you have sickness in your body that means you have not enough truth, theirs a truth that you don't understand to be set free. Yeshua is the truth, next example saints John 9:3 As He passed along, He noticed a man blind from his birth.2 His disciples asked Him, Rabbi, who sinned, this man or his parents, that he should be born blind? 3 Jesus answered, it was not that this man or his parents sinned, but he was born blind in order that the workings of God should be manifested (displayed and illustrated) in him. The understanding was not Just Yeshua, it was truth, He is the way the truth and the light, Yehsua walked in so much truth, he can say to anyone be thou made whole and heal anyone. When you walk in the understanding of his word and divine revelation sickness is not allowed in your body, Practice the word and speak his word more than your own talk day and night.

Saints let's move on, Revelation 20:20 Then I saw an angel descending from heaven; he was holding the key of the Abyss (the bottomless pit) and a great chain was in his hand.2 And he gripped *and* overpowered the dragon, that old serpent [of primeval times], who is the devil and Satan, and [securely] bound him for a thousand years.3 Then he hurled him into the Abyss (the bottomless pit) and closed it and sealed it above him, so that he should no longer lead astray *and* deceive *and* seduce the nations until the thousand years were at an end. After that he must be liberated for a short time. Didn't Yeshua state when we overcome we shall rule nations, are we rulings nations yet, point two what is the (Chain) resemble his word, the mysteries and secrets of the kingdom. We will have the power to Bind Satan and all his army for 1,000 years reign, in the new millennium here and now coming to fruition.

OK Saints here is some more, According to Scientific intelligence every seven years you get a whole new set of cells in your body, scientists are still trying to figure out why do people die then or age, there still trying to find that DNA in us. If we get a new set of cells every 7years, new cells, why are we aging, because we're not supposed too. Adam and Eve and Enoch Methuselah etc. lived how long, yes Hundreds of years many generations. That means when you get more of the truth and his word of Divine revelations in you in your DNA of his word you will enter back into your Glorified body immortality.

1 Timothy 5 18 For the Scripture says, you shall not muzzle an ox when it is treading out the grain, and again, the laborer is worthy of his hire. Don't shut up the Apostolic teaching, while it's treading out the grain, treading the ground which is earth, which means us, planting seeds within us also while he is plowing and reaping out the secrets of divine understanding, shredding and opening of the veils. Grain means food, the manna the mysteries the secret apostolic parables. There is a difference between Pastors seeds and The Apostles and Prophets Seeds. A Pastor, Evangelist, Teacher, Bishop, Reverend, Deacon cannot teach you the Book of Revelation. Everyone thinks it's the End of the world no it's a love letter to the Bride. There are symbolisms in the Book of Revelation, every Revelation is a Manifestation. Judgment means in Hebrew, Purification and also literally means when I don't understand something, he comes to discipline me and teach me to what I didn't understand. Judgment does not mean the end of the world. Judgment can be good or bad, Rod means yoke, teaching, spare the teaching and spoil the child. The churches have spoiled us and not taught us how we should.

There are many Fallen Teachers that have written books, you should not even desecrate your own house to contain such books and hear and listen to the false teachings all over the Air with these great Titles they carry, there are strong web filters like spider webs attaching them to your spirit, your clothes, your robes. Which does what, it creates magma a solid crystallized form like an egg, poison eggs, and false impregnation. Just like food poison that needs to be digested and come out, but this severity cannot come out cause you continue to feed it. So what does this mean you need to untwist your teachings of what you been taught. In the Book of Exodus 13:13 so it was that quails came up at evening and covered the camp, and in the morning the dew lay all around the camp. 14 And when the layer of dew lifted, there, on the surface of the wilderness, was a small round substance, *as* fine as frost on the ground. The morning dew was the Breath of Yah His Presence, breathing his life and character in us. Layer means in Hebrew (Copulation-Intercourse) the seed of which is the word of Yah, it lifted in Hebrew means to ascend (Ala) means rapture in Hebrew. When your being caught up with revelation and understanding. Yah told John the revelator to come up here in the spirit realm up on high the mystery and secrets of the Kingdom, small in Hebrew means to (Crush-Mortar), seeds are placed in a stone Mortar, a stone cup, the stone pestle is moved around the cup to crush the seeds into powder. In the bible it states Ezekiel 16:13 A new heart also will I give you, and a new spirit will I put within you: and I will take away the (stony heart) out of your flesh, and I will give you and heart of flesh.

Matthew 21:44 and whosoever shall fall on this stone shall be broken: but on whomsoever it shall fall, it will grind him to powder. Rapture means God's Wrath, his discipline of his pressure and tribulations for you to change your ways. It's his mercy being poured out on you, Frost means in Hebrew to cover a lid (Atonement his Seat of Mercy) Yah's manna to reconcile to repent and forgive. The end of age and rapture is not about leaving this earth, it's about Yah's mercy, and Covering is also a pitch, which also meant the Ark Noah's ark so he wouldn't sink in the water the flood. So what is the Ark of the Covenant being pitched, it's the shutting of the holes within us so his Glory will not be leaked out.

As I explained in my second book about the Tithe, The Fruits of Favor and Increase page 82 & 83. Malachi 3:10 Bring ye all the tithes into the storehouse, that there may be meat in mine house, and prove me now herewith, saith the LORD of hosts, if I will not open you the windows of heaven, and pour you out a blessing, that there shall not be room enough to receive it.11 And I will rebuke the devourer for your sakes, and he shall not destroy the fruits of your ground; neither shall your vine cast her fruit before the time in the field, saith the LORD of hosts.

Tithe means one tenth of a whole, Eyeh Asher Eyeh wants all of you wholeheartedly, and 1st commandment love the Heavenly Father with all your heart mind and soul. Storehouse means (You-You're the Temple of the Holy spirit-You're the Tabernacle) Where was the Ark of the Covenant the Holy of Holies, outer court, Inner court, Holy of Holies. Meat means revelation his mysteries, secrets the correct teachings and understanding of his word. The Apostle Paul said, 1 Corinthians 18 for the message of the cross is foolishness to those who are perishing, but to us who are being saved it is the power of God. 19 for it is written:" I will destroy the wisdom of the wise, and bring to nothing the understanding of the prudent."[A]

20 Where *is* the wise? Where *is* the scribe? Where *is* the disputer of this age? Has not God made foolish the wisdom of this world? 21 For since, in the wisdom of God, the world through wisdom did not know God, it pleased God through the foolishness of the message preached to save those who believe. 22 For Jews request a sign, and Greeks seek after wisdom; 23 but we preach Christ crucified, to the Jews a stumbling block and to the Greeks[b] foolishness, 24 but to those who are called, both Jews and Greeks, Christ the power of God and the wisdom of God.

25 Because the foolishness of God is wiser than men, and the weakness of God is stronger than men.

Where is the self-exalted fool who practices lawlessness and pretends to be teachers of the Mosaic law, where's is the False Prophets and carnal Christians who have received the teaching of the fallen angels impregnated unto man to seduce and twist his word, where is the Litigator of this so called New World Order of deception and Rapture of the end of this world coming to an end.

26 For you see your calling, brethren, that not many wise according to the flesh, not many mighty, not many noble, *are called.* 27 But God has chosen the foolish things of the world to put to shame the wise, and God has chosen the weak things of the world to put to shame the things which are mighty; 28 and the base things of the world and the things which are despised God has chosen, and the things which are not, to bring to nothing the things that are, 29 that no flesh should glory in His presence. 30 But of Him you are in Christ Jesus, who became for us wisdom from God—and righteousness and sanctification and redemption— 31 that, as it is written, "He who glories, let him glory in the Lord."[c] Not many can understand the deeps things of Yah!

1 Corinthians Chap 2:2 And I, brethren, when I came to you, did not come with excellence of speech or of wisdom declaring to you the testimony[d] of God. 2 For I determined not to know anything among you except Jesus Christ and Him crucified. 3 I was with you in weakness, in fear, and in much trembling. 4 And my speech and my preaching *were* not with persuasive words of human[e] wisdom, but in demonstration of the Spirit and of power, 5 that your faith should not be in the wisdom of men but in the power of God. Where is the Demonstration of the

Power of the Holy Spirit within you and in your apostolic church buildings? I was with you in weakness (trials and tribulations of discipline) in fear with much reverence of Yah within me glorying him only, much trembling the father blazing furnace of his presence within me. Jeremiah 20:7 [But Jeremiah said] O Lord, You have persuaded *and* deceived me, and I was persuaded *and* deceived; You are stronger than I am and You have prevailed. I am a laughingstock all the day; everyone mocks me.

8 For whenever I speak, I must cry out *and* complain; I shout, Violence and destruction! For the word of the Lord has become to me a reproach and a derision *and* has brought me insult all day long.

9 If I say, I will not make mention of [the Lord] or speak any more in His name, in my mind *and* heart it is as if there were a burning fire shut up in my bones. And I am weary of enduring *and* holding it in; I cannot [contain it any longer].

1 Corinthians 2:6 however, we speak wisdom among those who are mature, yet not the wisdom of this age, nor of the rulers of this age, who are coming to nothing. 7 But we speak the wisdom of God in a mystery, the hidden *wisdom* which God ordained before the ages for our glory, 8 which none of the rulers of this age knew; for had they known, they would not have crucified the Lord of glory.

9 But as it is written: "Eye has not seen, nor ear heard, nor have entered into the heart of man, the things which God has prepared for those who love Him."[f] It's a mystery to understand the deep things of Yah. Ruler means also a teacher, scribe one who lays out the foundation of his word by parables, line upon line, precept upon precept, like a ruler measurement stick.

10 But God has revealed *them* to us through His Spirit. For the Spirit searches all things, yes, and the deep things of God. 11 For what man knows the things of a man accept the spirit of the man which is in him? Even so no one knows the things of God except the Spirit of God. 12 Now we have received, not the spirit of the world, but the Spirit who is from God, that we might know the things that have been freely given to us by God.

13 These things we also speak, not in words which man's wisdom teaches but which the Holy[g] Spirit teaches, comparing spiritual things with spiritual. 14 But the natural man does not receive the things of the Spirit of God, for they are foolishness to him; nor can he know *them,* because they are spiritually discerned. 15 But he who is spiritual judges all things, yet he himself is *rightly* judged by no one. 16 For "who has known the mind of the LORD that he may instruct Him?"[h] But we have the mind of Christ.

1 Corinthians 3:3 And I, brethren, could not speak to you as to spiritual *people* but as to carnal, as to babes in Christ. 2 I fed you with milk and not with solid food; for until now you were not able *to receive it,* and even now you are still not able; 3 for you are still carnal. For where *there are* envy, strife, and divisions among you, are you not carnal and behaving like *mere* men? 4 For when one says, "I am of Paul," and another, "I *am* of Apollos," are you not carnal? I fed you milk and not Meat which is Solid Food you could not understand it. Back to Malachi Scripture meat, in my storehouse, you are the store house (Your temple that stores and applies his teachings within you) when there is meat in your storehouse within you not just milk. See that I will not open the windows of heaven, windows resemble in Hebrew (metaphor of eyes) also

lattice a framework, when your eyes are unveiled from the cataracts of the false, The Fathers specific framework oh how he works out your purpose and destiny come to alignment, his frame work is constructed within you in his divine plan. It continues see that I will not pour out a blessing that you do not have room enough to handle. Now does it say he leaks it out, leaks means you have holes, pouring when you drink a cup of water you're in balance and constructed correctly it doesn't leak. So his glory is not polluted or leaked out of you. When you have leaks or cracks that means other things can enter.

It continues to say Malachi 3: 11 And I will rebuke the devourer [insects and plagues] for your sakes and he shall not destroy the fruits of your ground, neither shall your vine drop its fruit before the time in the field, says the Lord of hosts. Insects are ungodly soul ties that harm your crops and curse you in the spirit. Plagues are false teachings (witchery, human spirits, and false prophecies). It continues to say it will not destroy the fruits of your ground, it will not allow your characteristics and personalities, your motive and intentions of your heart be polluted within you, when you receive religion, compromise, complacency not growing. You begin to deny Christ within you when your fruit of his character is polluted within you. Casting your fruits, your gifts and talents with your heart also for private gain deceitfulness, no transparency, prostituting one another, selling one another for personal private gain. Ground means earth your habitation, your upbringing, it also means you within you, and you're made of dust of the earth. Who is the Vine (Yeshua Christ within you) he is the vine we are the branches, neither shall your vine drop its fruits, prostitution, selling it, allowing your gifts and talents with your fruit of character compromising the word for self-gain, prostituting your yourself. Neither shall your vine drop its fruit before the time, time in Hebrew means (Assembly) when you assemble amongst others, when you assemble with the Elite or other generals or carnal Christians with highly intellectual warfare of icons of psychology and psychological as semblance. You won't drop the ball or be influenced with their witchery of sound doctrine, you will be spiritually discerned, not letting something else pour in you, and you will not prostitute yourself. The Field means in Hebrew (Absolute-Heart) also means the ministry work, Shedemah (Field) -of uncertain derivation -. The obtaining or developing of something from a source or origin.

CHAPTER 7

What is being developed in your heart from what source, source in Hebrew means maqor (a spring, fountain), are you receiving from the Spirit of Yeshua of living waters, or are you receiving it from 1 Corinthians 10: Ye cannot drink the cup of the Lord, and the cup of devils: ye cannot be partakers of the Lord's table, and of the table of devils.

Job 1:6 now there was a day when the sons of God came to present themselves before the LORD, and Satan came also among them. There was an assembly wasn't there, there was an elite of generals of sons or angels, no one could perceive he was there only Yeshua himself. There is a gift called Discerning of spirits, its apart of Yeshuas Framework. Origin in Hebrew mekurah means (a place of digging out) also meaning what are you digging into, also or mkorah {mek-o-raw'}; from the same as kuwr in the sense of dipping; origin (as if a mine) -- birth, habitation, nativity. What are you digging into or what needs to be dugged out of you, what are you dipping into, what being birthed out of you and also what is being inhabited within you. Habitation means in Hebrew meadows, pleasant place, or also Psalms 23:2 He lets me rest in green meadows; he leads me beside peaceful streams. So theoretically speaking you can see yourself of the surroundings you're in, you can see, perceive and understand what's being taught to you. So also its meaning what is it you cannot see that's there. The answer is worship Saints, what you cannot perceive understand, your circumstances situations, what's within you, or cannot receive his framework just worship him in spirit and in truth. Truthfully and wholeheartedly.

Psalms 32:7 Thou art my hiding-place; thou wilt preserve me from trouble; Thou wilt compass me about with songs of deliverance. Saints let me give you the Final Revelation to the Tithe, James 5:7 be patient therefore, brethren, until the coming of the Lord. Behold, the husbandman waited for the precious fruit of the earth, being patient over it, until it receive the early and latter rain. The fruits are the seeds being planted by the Apostles and Prophets treading out the grain and given it out as food manna, both the early and latter rain. Giving you seeds to be impregnated by the word of revelation preparing for the Bridegroom, to give birth to the Apostolic God Head within you. The seed is the word, the seed that goes in the ground earth you, when the earth manifests the seed, which then Harvest the grain(Former Rain),animals(Beasts of the Earth-Carnality) then Fruits(The Latter Rain). Now when the fruits come forth (Character Conduct) you bring an offering which also resembles a sacrifice unto Yah.

Malachi 3:10 Bring ye the whole tithe into the store-house, that there may be food in my house, and prove me now herewith, smith Jehovah of hosts,(if I will not open you the windows of heaven, and pour you out a blessing, that there shall not be room enough to receive it).

So when you offer up an offering of yourselves as the good fruit, you are caught up, you go up into smoke, when you move into his presence of Yah caught up in the heavens in a Realm up of Glory he covers your sins and protects you. This is a place and the Realm of his Glory that the enemy cannot enter in. There is no room for Spiritual Warfare, only the Holy Spirit leads you to spiritual warfare by an unction. There is complete Confidence in the Holy Spirit doing the job. So when you become Smoke you're a sweet smell to his Nostrils, filled with Revelation and understanding. Philippians 4:18 But I have received everything in full and have an abundance; I am amply supplied, having received from Epaphroditus what you have sent, a fragrant aroma, an acceptable sacrifice, well-pleasing to God. 2 Corinthians 2:14 But thanks be to God, who always leads us in triumph in Christ, and manifests through us the sweet aroma of the knowledge of Him in every place. For we are a fragrance of Christ to God among those who are being saved and among those who are perishing; to the one an aroma from death to death, to the other an aroma from life to life and who is adequate for these things?

Then what does a cloud do?" it rains, so then you can become a light unto the world. You will have the ability when to bring it out or shut up the heavens within you by the leading of the Holy Spirit. You become the Pillar and the Cloud of His Shekinah Glory (Shamayin). You then become the dew unto this earth, you also begin to pour out what's been giving to you. Genesis 27:28 May God give you heaven's dew and earth's richness-- an abundance of grain and new wine. What fragrance are you to the father Eyeh Asher Eyeh Isaiah 65:5Yet they say to each other, 'Don't come too close or you will defile me! I am holier than you!' These people are a stench in my nostrils, an acrid smell that never goes away.

Isaiah 1:13 the incense you bring me is a stench in my nostrils! Your celebrations of the new moon and the Sabbath day, and your special days for fasting -- even your most pious meetings -- are all sinful and false. I want nothing more to do with them. 14 I hate all your festivals and sacrifices. I cannot stand the sight of them! 15 From now on, when you lift up your hands in prayer, I will refuse to look. Even though you offer many prayers, I will not listen. For your hands are covered with the blood of your innocent victims. 16 Wash yourselves and be clean! Let me no longer see your evil deeds. Give up your wicked ways. 17 Learn to do well. Seek justice. Help the oppressed. Defend the orphan. Fight for the rights of widows. 18 "Come now, let us argue this out," says the LORD. "No matter how deep the stain of your sins, I can remove it. I can make you as clean as freshly fallen snow. Even if you are stained as red as crimson, I can make you as white as wool. 19 If you will only obey me and let me help you, then you will have plenty to eat. 20 But if you keep turning away and refusing to listen, you will be destroyed by your enemies. I, the LORD, have spoken!" 21 See how Jerusalem, once so faithful, has become a prostitute. Once the home of justice and righteousness, she is now filled with murderers. 22 Once like pure silver, you have become like worthless slag. Once so pure, you are now like watered-down wine. 23 Your leaders are rebels, the companions of thieves. All of them take bribes and refuse to defend the orphans and the widows.

OK Saints watch this, Malachi 3:3 Behold, I will send my messenger, and he shall prepare the way before me: and the LORD, whom ye seek, shall (suddenly) come to his temple, even the messenger of the covenant, whom ye delight in: behold, he shall come, saith the LORD of hosts.2 But who may abide the day of his coming? And who shall stand when he appeareth? for he is like a refiner's fire, and like fullers' soap:3 And he shall sit as a refiner and purifier of silver: and he shall purify the sons of Levi, and purge them as gold and silver, that they may offer unto the LORD an offering in righteousness. You become an offering of Righteousness. The father Yah is saying what kind of offering you are making them into, what kind of preparation is being birthed within the inside. Isaiah 66:20 And they shall bring all your brethren for an offering unto the LORD out of all nations upon horses, and in chariots, and in litters, and upon mules, and upon swift beasts, to my holy mountain Jerusalem, saith the LORD, as the children of Israel bring an offering in a clean vessel into the house of the LORD.21 And I will also take of them for priests and for Levites, saith the LORD.

You notice in Malachi 2:7 For the priest's lips should keep knowledge, and they should seek the law at his mouth; for he is the messenger of the LORD of hosts.8 But ye have departed from the way; ye have caused many to stumble at the law; ye have corrupted the covenant of Levi," saith the LORD of hosts.9 "Therefore have I also made you contemptible and base before all the people, according as ye have not kept My ways but have been partial in the law." Saints it just stated the priests have been only in partial of the Law, Tithe means portion (Tenth), also tenth of a whole, complete reverence not partial.

Malachi 3:8 Will a man rob God? Yet ye have robbed me! But ye say, 'Wherein have we robbed Thee?' In tithes and offerings. Not to be showing partiality in Eyeh Asher Eyehs teachings halfheartedly (False teachings of Doctrine), offering also. Watch this Saints Romans 6:6 knowing this, that our old man was crucified with him, that the body of sin might be done away, that so we should no longer be in bondage to sin; 7 for he that hath died is justified from sin.9 knowing that Christ being raised from the dead dieth no more; death no more hath dominion over him. 12 Let not sin therefore reign in your mortal body, that ye should obey the lusts thereof: 13 neither present your members unto sin as instruments of unrighteousness; but present yourselves unto God, as alive from the dead, and your members as instruments of righteousness unto God.14 For sin shall not have dominion over you: for ye are not under law, but under grace.

Listen Carefully and hear what the spirit is saying, 19 I speak after the manner of men because of the infirmity of your flesh: for as ye presented your members as servants to uncleanness and to iniquity unto iniquity, even so now present your members as servants to righteousness unto sanctification.20 For when ye were servants of sin, ye were free in regard of righteousness.21 What (fruit) then had ye at that time in the things whereof ye are now ashamed? For the end of those things is death.22 but now being made free from sin and become servants to God, ye have your (fruit) unto sanctification, and the end eternal life. Wow you just read word for word Fruit of character, conduct, Sanctification, or bad fruit, sin, lust, iniquity etc.

Jeremiah 2:20 "Long ago you broke off your yoke and tore off your bonds; you said, 'I will not serve you!' Indeed, on every high hill and under every spreading tree you lay down as a prostitute.21 I had planted you like a choice vine of sound and reliable stock. How then did you turn against me into a corrupt, wild vine?22 Although you wash yourself with soap and use an abundance of cleansing powder, the stain of your guilt is still before me, "declares the Sovereign LORD. The book Of Malachi also speaks as a choice vine, a firm tree and a Prostitute, selling yourself s for self-gain. It also states reliable stock In Hebrew Mahpeketh: stocks (instrument of punishment), (compelling *crooked* posture, or *distorting*). Distorting the truth miss interpretation of the Book of Malachi about Tithe and Offering.

Romans 15:16 [16] that I should be the minister of Jesus Christ to the Gentiles, ministering the Gospel of God, that the offering up of the Gentiles might be acceptable, being sanctified by the Holy Ghost. We become the offering of Sacrifice unto him alone. Have a purified heart, body, mind, soul and spirit cleansed completely. Romans 14: [17] [After all] the kingdom of God is not a matter of [getting the] food and drink [one likes], but instead it is righteousness (that state which makes a person acceptable to God) and [heart] peace and joy in the Holy Spirit.

How can Tithe of 10 Percent please my father in heaven and they say I'm under covenant if I do, if my heart is not pure or if my spirit and my will not sanctified and lead by the Holy Spirit. We need to die completely to self and receive self-revelation of ourselves to be set free.

John 6:55 My flesh is true food and my blood is true drink. False doctrine sanitizes his word and deludes of its true meaning with spirits involved such as the spirit of Abaddon which is Apollyon. This revelation is explained in my 4th book.

Suddenly in ancient Hebrew suddenly and instantly, opening of the eye in a moment, in a wink of time. 1 Corinthians 15:42 It is the same way with the resurrection of the dead. Our earthly bodies are planted in the ground when we die, but they will be raised to live forever. 43 Our bodies are buried in brokenness, but they will be raised in glory. They are buried in weakness, but they will be raised in strength. 44 They are buried as natural human bodies, but they will be raised as spiritual bodies. For just as there are natural bodies, there are also spiritual bodies.

45 The Scriptures tell us, "The first man, Adam, became a living person."[h] But the last Adam—that is, Christ—is a life-giving Spirit. 46 What comes first is the natural body, then the spiritual body comes later. 47 Adam, the first

man, was made from the dust of the earth, while Christ, the second man, came from heaven. 48 Earthly people are like the earthly man, and heavenly people are like the heavenly man. 49 Just as we are now like the earthly man, we will someday be like [I] the heavenly man.

50 What I am saying, dear brothers and sisters, is that our physical bodies cannot inherit the Kingdom of God. These dying bodies cannot inherit what will last forever.

51 But let me reveal to you a wonderful secret. We will not all die, but we will all be transformed! 52 It will happen in a moment, in the blink of an eye, when the last trumpet (Apostle Prophets speaking in mystery revelations) is blown. For when the trumpet sounds, those who have died will be raised to live forever. And we who are living will also be transformed. 53 For our dying bodies must be transformed into bodies that will never die; our mortal bodies must be transformed into immortal bodies.

Resurrection in Hebrew means, moral aspect of redefining or recovery of spiritual truth, you cannot have a resurrection without a recovery of your own mindsets through revelation of his word and understand it when your being circumcised then you will understand. Sown in Greek Spiro means metaphorically a proverbial saying, same as a parable of the word of God. When you understand the Parables and secrets and mysteries, you will receive a resurrection immortal body back into once was the Garden of Eden.

1 Corinthians 2:6 Yet when I am among mature believers, I do speak with words of wisdom, but not the kind of wisdom that belongs to this world or to the rulers of this world, who are soon forgotten. 7 No, the wisdom we speak of is the mystery of God—his plan that was previously

hidden, even though he made it for our ultimate glory before the world began. 8 But the rulers of this world have not understood it; if they had, they would not have crucified our glorious Lord. 9 That is what the Scriptures mean when they say, "No eye has seen, no ear has heard, and no mind has imagined what God has prepared for those who love him." It stated no one has seen, heard, no mind had imagined what he has prepared for us!

Now let me clarify some more revelation interpretation of this Tabernacle age coming here and now. Hebrews 9:8 The Holy Ghost this signifying, that the way into the holiest of all was not yet made manifest, while as the first tabernacle was yet standing: Yahweh is saying no one has fully went in the realm of what he has prepared for us until now, (The full complete symbolic parable and teachings the way into the Holiest of all).!9 Which was a figure for the time then present, in which were offered both gifts and sacrifices that could not make him that did the service perfect, as pertaining to the conscience. It states it was a figure (Greek means Parable-Mystery a Secret-Revelation) something you cannot imagine to your own conscience. It was only Symbolic for our time here and now! The Torah is where you see the Symbolism of Revelation of understanding.

OK let me give you some more symbolism a woman named Zena Whitcombe a diagram of the Model of Transition through the Consciousness Time Zone. Scientists or the smartest brains of our time state we have 100 billion Neurons, when we look at these Neurons through a magnifying scope there are Diamond Shaped Clusters. Further we have 600 trillion synapses that act as flex compositors (Just like the movie back to the Future the Flex Compositor was the component for the vehicle).

Meaning we have more firing signals in the brain more than all the galaxies and everything out there in space. This is How the Diagram look likes. I am not considering the fact that the bottom diagram is the truth or making any standards that it is true. The bottom diagram I am just given you a symbolic symbol that someone came up with the Adamic age, of a higher conscious zone since 1977. Everything that was given to me through teachings of other Apostles and Prophets even yes regular servants who just studied the torah, and reveal or unveiled these mysteries and secrets to what we are speaking of. The Tabernacle age, Kingdom age a higher form of existence that was never been birthed or released until now. I am speaking on this symbolism on the bottom graph because it gives some understanding to the mystery I speak of.

Genesis 3:24 So he drove out the man; and he placed at the east of the garden of Eden Cherubim s, and a flaming sword which turned every way, to keep the way of the tree of life. Flaming in Ancient lexicon Hebrew means-1262) (לתה LTh) AC: Cover CO: Veil AB: Secret. Yahweh, Yeshua and the Holy Spirit is given us the Keys to go back to once was the Garden of Eden, it was made for our time here and now. Yeshua came to restore all things hello that means everything. OK Saints let me give you some Insight to this mystery, Have you or any of you watched the movie the Book of Eli, by Denzel Washington. The movie is about the King James Bible. Here is a phrase stated by the Actor Gary Goldman-Carnige the Evil Mobster of the Town. Eli escapes somehow from a locked room, Carnige states we need that book, one gentlemen gets all mad cause and stated it's just a book. Carnegie screams out in frustration and anger stating (We need that book, it's a weapon and a tool, to the hearts and souls and minds of the weak and destitute) the whole world of people will come to this deserted place if we have it. We will be able to control them and do whatever we tell them what to do by having that book with its words.

What do you think it's happening all over the world, no disrespect to anyone here, but some or little or most have enormous amounts of ignorance inside you and no one can't tell you or help you understand what's really happening in your congregation or your church. Well because you're bored, lonely, you want to feel appreciated, a lot of people in there you think it has good fruit, your hiding behind your own insecurity issues, there is nothing else for you to do. The mere fact of being alone, and cannot trust God to give you true friendship people you can trust. You will accept anything or anyone no matter how it looks like, you have no discernment, no understanding, you will do anything to get plugged into somewhere and you think there really your family. With all the rules and regulations of Spiritual Witchcraft they feed you, in false humility, false love but keep Tithing and sowing your Seed of Money to them. They own you and your family, and even control your own household you dwell in even though there not living there. Here is one of the greatest instructions I can offer you, Ask The Holy Spirit or Eyeh Asher Eyeh, Yeshua to show you the motive and intentions of their hearts, of the people your involved with, family, and even you church leaders!. Also if you would consider asking him to show you or give you a Self-Revelation of yourself!

CHAPTER 8

Saints beneath you is a photo of consideration explanation of scientific sense. Most people try how to understand how we are going to be upheld or grasp the understanding the transitional phase of immortality.

This pic is just an ironic or symbolism of justification. The bottom pic expresses some key points in symbolism's like, Scientists have already explained we have 100 billion neurons and states when look at bio-microscopically they look like Diamond Clusters.

They state also we have 60 to 100 trillion synapses that act like Flex compositors in a sense. Well ironically this photo resembles a diamond shaped cluster, also you notice it has 9 dimensions of activity.

The bible Speaks of 9 fruits of the gifts of the spirit. Everyone or some or most think that the speed of light is the fastest form of speed, well muon waves is faster. Just giving out some symbolic references to ironic categorizes for explanation. Thank you all for spending the time of reading my books.

May Eyeh the Father get all the glory unto him thank you for everything? May Yeshua grant everyone's hearts desires. May Yeshua increase your territories, and all increase in all directions come your way in Yehsuas name. May his warring angels protect you and speak to you and guide you with the Holy Spirit. May all things come to fruition within the father divine will and promise upon your lives?

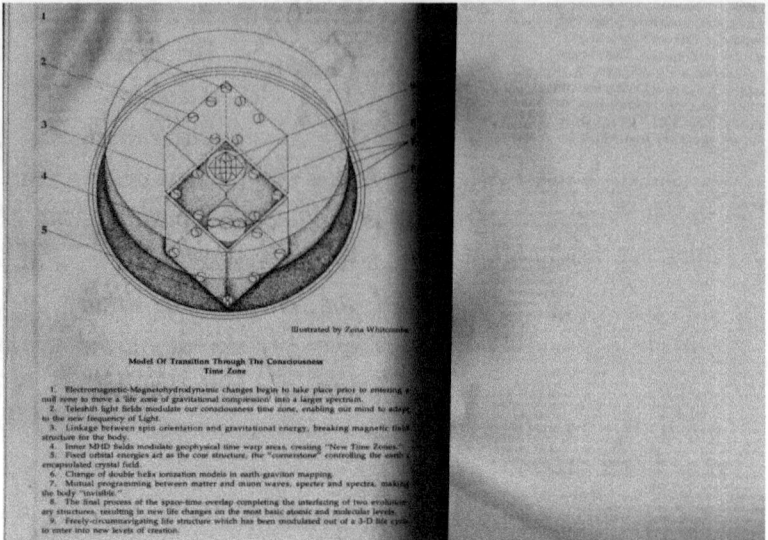

Model Of Transition Through The Consciousness
Time Zone

1. Electromagnetic-Magnetohydrodynamic changes begin to take place prior to entering a null zone to move a 'life zone' of gravitational compression' into a larger spectrum.
2. Teleshift light fields modulate our consciousness (time zone, enabling our mind to adapt to the new frequency of Light.
3. Linkage between spin orientation and gravitational energy, breaking magnetic field structure for the body.
4. Inner MHD fields modulate geophysical time warp areas, creating "New Time Zones."
5. Fixed orbital energies act as the core structure, the "cornerstone" controlling the earth's encapsulated crystal field.
6. Change of double helix ionization models in earth graviton mapping.
7. Mutual programming between matter and onion waves, specter and spectra, making the body "invisible."
8. The final process of the space-time overlap completing the interlacing of two evolutionary structures, resulting in new life changes on the most basic atomic and molecular levels.
9. Freely-circumnavigating life structure which has been modulated out of a 3-D life cycle to enter into new levels of creation.

Saints the Ridiculous Tribulation Rapture of being taken away is a marketing tactic of your Money, keeping you in fear and control. Obadiah1:20 and the captives of this host of the children of Israel shall possess that of the Canaanites, even unto Zarephath; and the captives of Jerusalem who are in Sepharad shall possess the cities of the south. 21 And saviors shall come up on Mount Zion to judge the mount of Esau; and the kingdom shall be the Lord's. Who were the Canaanites the Fallen Angels (The Nephilim's), we shall overcome and rule the Fallen angels of city and nations and governments,   Saints were not going nowhere. Only those who do not except this truth will die old decay and wax away or fall into their own corruption. Really next verse it says and Saviors (Who are the Saviors Us Saints) Christ in us the hope of Glory. We shall become Princes and above the Kings of the Earth and Angels. You do not become a Prince of Eyeh Asher Eyeh until you receive Universal Power, they shall inherit all things of Heaven and On Earth.

Finally the Spirit of Yah and his army has two side. In the bible He states I am the God of Heaven and Earth I create Evil and good. Which army are you part of, In the Bible God even states I trap man in his own wisdom, 1 Corinthians 3:19 For the wisdom of this world is foolishness to God. As the Scriptures say, "He traps the wise in the snare of their own cleverness." Revelation 9: **7**The locusts looked like horses prepared for battle. On their heads they wore something like crowns of gold, and their faces resembled human faces. **8**Their hair was like women's hair, and their teeth were like lions' teeth. **9**They had breastplates like breastplates of iron, and the sound of their wings was like the thundering of many horses and chariots rushing into battle. **10**They had tails with stingers, like scorpions, and in their tails they had power to torment people for five months. **11**They had as king over them the angel of the Abyss, whose name in Hebrew is Abaddon and in Greek is Apollyon (that is, Destroyer).

You notice they had crown of gold on their heads and human faces this is Also Gods Army that was deceived by their own selves or the false doctrine and spirits of Satan (Religious Doctrine). You notice also verse 10 they had power to torment people for five months, resembles apostolic church hurting or destroying their own kind also God's grace upon mankind. They were deceived by false spirit of Abaddon-Apollyon the Destroyer.

Revelation 9:12 The first woe is past; two other woes are yet to come. The Second woe is the Redemption of mankind and 7year revival and Inheritance of all what we been waiting for. Also the third woe is becoming immortal one with our father. Woe also means a transition or shift

103

of great grandeur of bad and good. Revelation 21:3 And I heard a great voice out of heaven saying, Behold, the tabernacle of God *is* with men, and he will dwell with them, and they shall be his people, and God himself shall be with them, *and be* their God. The Tabernacle of God is about to be enthroned within us!

13The sixth angel sounded his trumpet, and I heard a voice coming from the four horns of the golden altar that is before God. **14** It said to the sixth angel who had the trumpet, "Release the four angels who are bound at the great river Euphrates." **15** and the four angels who had been kept ready for this very hour and day and month and year were released to kill a third of mankind. **16** The number of the mounted troops was twice ten thousand times ten thousand. I heard their number.

17The horses and riders I saw in my vision looked like this: Their breastplates were fiery red, dark blue, and yellow as sulfur. The heads of the horses resembled the heads of lions, and out of their mouths came fire, smoke and sulfur. **18**A third of mankind was killed by the three plagues of fire, smoke and sulfur that came out of their mouths. **19**The power of the horses was in their mouths and in their tails; for their tails were like snakes, having heads with which they inflict injury.

Dark blue water river of God, cleansing life giving flow of the Holy Spirit, the Word ruler ship, unlimited potential, priesthood(Esther 8:15) Red blood of Jesus, atonement, grace. Yellow joy, revelation. Saints verse 17 mouths came fire Prophecy, smoke the dew of Heaven his Presence and sulfur brimstone also means to Purify the Heart!. Also the had tails like snakes, be sharp as a serpent soft as a dove, having heads to inflict injury, Hebrews 4: For the word of God is alive and active. Sharper than any double-edged sword, it penetrates even to dividing soul and spirit, joints and marrow; it judges the thoughts and attitudes of the heart.

20The rest of mankind who were not killed by these plagues still did not repent of the work of their hands; they did not stop worshiping demons, and idols of gold, silver, bronze, stone and wood—idols that cannot see or hear or walk. **21**Nor did they repent of their murders, their magic arts, their sexual immorality or their thefts.

Saints the illustration of such interpretations are so divine we need to seek the father face to face and understood his proper timing in all things. Ecclesiastes 8:5 "A wise man's heart discerneth both time and judgment." Isaiah 50:4 the lord God has given me the tongue of the learned, that I should know how to speak a word in season to him is weary. The proper timing and leading of the Holy Spirit, we need to understand the orchestration of the leading of the Holy Spirit not just the Gift within us. Most people think just because they see gifts it's the orchestrations of the leading of the Holy Spirit, not knowing it's not the presence of God. Most ministries move in a spirit called racing sprit with their gifts, in convenience. Revelation must be released in accuracy of time. Any time the Holy Spirit speaks it belongs in a sequence of His timing.

Saints a great book to read by Prophet Robert Liardon, Spiritual timing printed 1990 25 years ago, he was in spirit when he wrote this small little book. He explained the malfunction in ministry that is still going on today big time!

ANTHONY MONTOYA

About The Author

Hello family, I'm just going to give you a brief illustration of my testimony about me and my life In Yahshua. I'm currently divorced over 10 years one daughter, my daughter is 13 one of the greatest life's experiences in my life. My parents are Ministers of the good news for the last 45years experience in the prophetic call and commission. My father's an Apostle and my mother's a Prophetess, who's been used for 17 years. I've been trained under the Holy Spirit and will always be in training, ever since my walk I've been taught to die to self and to lay down my own self will for the sake of the Kingdom for transformation. My biological father left me when I was 11, I had an encounter with God himself, the Father when I was 18 years of age.

One day everyone was gone, my mother had three children I am the middle child, it was around midnight walking around my home. I spoke to myself and stated I was all alone then the phone rang it was weird, then I said hello the voice said" Are you alone" I then said who is this. The voice continued and said "This is your Father, your not alone." Then I said, "ok who is this, stop playing around!" The voice continued and said, "Go to the mirror and then stated are you alone?" Then I said, "Who is this the voice?" Then he continued, "This is your Father Heaven." I was stunned for that moment and couldn't grasp or understand the situation and my brain went blank.

Since that day, I've been divorced ten years, slept in the streets homeless for about 6 years, kicked out of churches for being too prophetic, slept in houses with ministers who are apostles and prophets that astro projected out of their bodies.

While I have disobeyed Yahweh several times, he allowed me to see the demonic realm and was attacked heavily by my own disobedience, also by other leaders that have mastered the gift inside them using for their own self gain. Trained under the gift of the discerning of spirits, to discern the motive and intents of the hearts of the people around me.

I was just recently pulled out from being homeless, several years ago about 2 ½ to be precise, generational curses broken off from biological father who made a deal with Satan, An apostle prophesied and stated your biological father made a deal with Satan to have the blood of two of his children for promise for money for the rest of his life. My sister was cured from whooping cough there was no cure at that time. I was set free from several demonic spirits that are so real. My walk in ministry was to discern why so much division, only by Yahshua's grace and the Holy Spirit has graced me to understand the spirit of influence & religion using venom of false doctrine and false prophecies that's been impregnated in the hearts of gods children & have been left crippled and shuts down their own immune system.

My present state I'm ordained minister, my belief is to be a life living sacrifice for Yahweh's kingdom , only to be servant to others and help one another reach Yahweh's purpose n destiny in our lives. To unveil the mysteries and revelations of this kingdom age for all his children to be set free from religion, jezebel spirits, spirit of influence, psychology, false hope (false prophesies), rejection, abandonment guilt, shame, control, seared conscious, subconscious, conscious, mesmoratic cells, trauma, familiar spirits, camellia spirits that transforms and changes color, cockatrice spirit, the false god of Prosperity, Fortune & Destiny, mystical influences that general spirits have had dominion over us.

Isaiah 26: 13-14 (AMP) says, " O Lord, our God, other masters besides You have ruled over us, but we will acknowledge *and* mention Your name only.[14] They [the former tyrant masters] are dead, they shall not live *and* reappear; they are powerless ghosts, they shall not rise *and* come back. Therefore You have visited and made an end of them and caused every memory of them [every trace of their supremacy] to perish." This reference speaks of general demonic spirits even with all religious practices, he will even wipe away the memory of them out of us.

Anthony Montoya

BOOKS BY ANTHONY MONTOYA

The Seed Of Resurrection

The Fruits Of Favor And Increase

Apocalypse Encrypted! Revelation Unleashed!

Apocalypse Encrypted! Revelation Unleashed! – 2

MINISTRY CONTACT INFORMATION

You may contact Anthony Montoya

through the following sources:

Email Address:

Judah1231@yahoo.com

Website:

anthonymontoyas1.weebly.com